The Development of Self-Regulation in Latinx Preschool Children

Yolanda Medina and Margarita Machado-Casas
Series Editors

Vol. 30

Ruth Guirguis and Raquel Plotka

The Development of Self-Regulation in Latinx Preschool Children

Theory, Research, and Applications

PETER LANG
New York · Berlin · Bruxelles · Chennai · Lausanne · Oxford

Library of Congress Cataloging-in-Publication Control Number: 2023033530

Bibliographic information published by the Deutsche Nationalbibliothek.
The German National Library lists this publication in the German
National Bibliography; detailed bibliographic data is available
on the Internet at http://dnb.d-nb.de.

Cover design by Peter Lang Group AG

ISSN 2372-6822 (print) ISSN 2372-6830 (online)
ISBN 9781636673387 (paperback)
ISBN 9781636673394 (ebook)
ISBN 9781636673400 (epub)
DOI 10.3726/b21127

© 2024 Peter Lang Group AG, Lausanne
Published by Peter Lang Publishing Inc., New York, USA
info@peterlang.com - www.peterlang.com

All rights reserved.
All parts of this publication are protected by copyright.
Any utilization outside the strict limits of the copyright law, without the permission of the
publisher, is forbidden and liable to prosecution.
This applies in particular to reproductions, translations, microfilming, and storage and
processing in electronic retrieval systems.

This publication has been peer reviewed.

DEDICATION

We would like to dedicate this book to our young Latinx community whose needs matter and to those advocates who contribute to raising awareness of Latinx children's regulatory exigencies.

CONTENTS

ACKNOWLEDGMENTS xi
INTRODUCTION xv

CHAPTER 1. EARLY CHILDHOOD PROGRAMS AND LATINX CHILDREN 1
Preschool Curricula Today 3
What Are *Familismo,* *Respeto,* and *Educación*? 5
The Growing Gap of Self-Regulatory Skills in Latinx Preschoolers 7

CHAPTER 2. THEORETICAL BACKGROUND: FOUCAULT AND VYGOTSKY 9
Institutional Power 10
"Regimes of Truth" 11
Knowledge and Power 12
Socialization in the Early Years 13
Zone of Proximal Development (ZPD) 14
Language 14

CHAPTER 3. SELF-REGULATION AND CRITICAL ASSOCIATIONS — 17
Self-Regulation — 18
Behavioral, Emotional, and Cognitive Regulation — 19
Self-Regulation and Language — 22
Self-Regulation and Social Skills — 23
Self-Regulation and Academic Achievement — 24
Self-Regulation and Emergent Literacy Skills — 25
Latinx Parenting, Self-Regulation, and Latinx Preschoolers — 28
Self-Regulation and Self-Assertion, Compliance, and Discipline — 29

CHAPTER 4. CURRENT DATA ON SELF-REGULATION IN LATINX PRESCHOOLERS — 35
Method — 36
Setting — 37
Procedures — 42
Results: Associations Between Latinx Preschoolers' Language Skills and Self-Regulation — 43
Analysis of Time 1 and Time 2 Results: Self-Regulation and Academic Achievement — 45
Analysis of Time 1 and Time 2 Results: Self-Regulation and Language Acquisition Skills — 46
What Do the Findings Mean? — 47
Results, Regimes of Truth, and Vygotsky — 49

CHAPTER 5. IMPLEMENTING SELF-REGULATION PRACTICES FOR LATINX PRESCHOOLERS — 51
Current Educational Policies — 52
Implications for Practice — 53
Language in the Latinx Preschool Classroom — 53
Social Interactions in the Latinx Preschool Classroom — 54
Play in the Latinx Preschool Classroom — 54
Cultural Awareness in the Latinx Preschool Classroom — 55
Assessing Latinx Children — 57
Preparing Teachers to be Multicultural Educators — 58

        Engaging Latinx Families in Early Childhood Programs   59
        Conclusion   63

CHAPTER 6. LESSONS LEARNED   67
        Lessons Learned by ECE Bilingual Educator
        Claritz Marte   68
        Lessons Learned by ECE Bilingual Intervention
        Specialist Laura Giolitti Egui   70
        Lessons Learned by ECE Higher Education Instructor
        Margaret Calabro   72

        AFTERWORD   75
        APPENDIX A   79
        APPENDIX B   85
        REFERENCES   87

ACKNOWLEDGMENTS

We sincerely thank our editor Dr. Yolanda (Jolie) Medina for her guidance and support throughout this process.

We would like to give the warmest and the most sincere thanks to all the wonderful teachers and children that contributed to the completion of this research.

Finally, we thank our students whose questions inspire us to continue to seek answers and improve practices.

Finally, we would like to acknowledge Southern Early Childhood Association for granting us permission to reproduce parts of the paper titled "Engaging Latino Families in Early Childhood Education Programs: Barriers, Misconceptions, and Recommendation" in chapter 5 which appeared originally in the *Dimensions in Early Childhood Education*, and to Common Ground Research Network for allowing us to reproduce parts of the paper titled "The Effects of Maternal Behaviors and Styles on the Development of Self-Assertion, Self-Regulation, Compliance, and Non-Compliance in Latino Toddlers" in chapter 3 which appeared originally in *The International Journal of Interdisciplinary Educational Studies*.

The Illustrators of this book are female Latinx artists that enjoy painting in different media as well as various digital art platforms. Elizabeth and Ariella designed the cover for this book based on their interpretation of the book's abstract. For Elizabeth, the effect of educational programs at a young age were the most impactful in her design. For Ariella, it was the implication of play as a form of learning that influenced her design.

INTRODUCTION

Ruth Guirguis

I vividly remember throwing down two inflatable mattresses in the family room and calling for my three little ones to come join me. They came running, excited about our upcoming sleeping adventure. I asked them, "What movie should we watch tonight?" They all enthusiastically responded, "The bee one!" I looked at my watch and saw that it was 6:00 p.m., and my heart started racing. My oldest would be going to kindergarten the following day, and I wanted to make the most of her last night before she embarked on her years ahead in formal school. But all I kept thinking was, "Where did the time go?" and "She is just not ready." That night, the words "She is not ready" repeatedly played in my head. The next morning, my daughter got up. As I dressed her, she asked, "Is today the new school?" I looked at her pretty curls, and I admired how much this sweet little girl had grown. I kissed her and reassured her, "You are going to love it!" She looked so sad and on the verge of tears but said, "Okay, mom." It was the longest and most silent eight-minute drive there. I could see how anxious she was as she pulled each of her fingers repeatedly.

As a parent of an entering kindergarten student, I had a rude awakening to what today's kindergarten curriculum entails. While, as a parent, my overall goals for her kindergarten school year were to make sure that my child did not have any separation anxiety and would meet a nurturing teacher who would foster in her a love of school. I wanted my child to develop the courage to take the bus alone to and from school, make friends on her own, and have the ability to regulate her behavior and emotions. By contrast, the school's focus was mainly on cognitive development. After only two months of school, during a parent-teacher conference, her teacher and a special education teacher (who was invited to the meeting without my knowledge) told me that my child was in need of push-in services and perhaps an evaluation, yet, no other key aspects of her development were addressed during this meeting. Her social and emotional domains did not seem to be of concern. Nor, her ability to manage and control her emotions. My refusal of all services struck them the wrong way, and they told me that they would communicate this information to the school principal. Weeks later, my daughter was pulled out of her classroom and taken to the principal's office. While at the principal's office and without any further explanation, she was given picture cards and asked to match the ones that rhymed. She failed. The principal brought it to my attention and suggested that we—I—should be doing more. I was lectured and asked if I knew the reputation of the school district I had moved into. It was an "academically rigorous school," the then-principal said, and in her time here, she "had never had a parent ask the school to leave their child alone." On the contrary, according to the principal, most parents request more work and rigor for their kids. The aspects of my daughter's emotional and social development, that fact she was struggling with many non-cognitive aspects of development, were not mentioned, nor, apparently, were they of concern to any of these adults to whom I had entrusted her education. At that moment, I realized that today's early childhood education only has room for academics, and the critical factors, such as socialization and self-regulation (which simply stating is self-control and contribute to the overall development of the kindergarten child), are unaccounted for in classrooms.

This experience led me to investigate the importance of the development of self-regulation in preschool students, specifically Latinx preschoolers such as my daughter. There is much literature on the importance of self-regulation and young learners, but there is a paucity of research in the field on the importance of self-regulation in Latinx preschoolers. Moreover, there is a dearth of quantitative data looking at Latinx preschoolers and regulatory skills.

This book focuses on quantitative data that was collected to explore the associations between self-regulation, academics, and Latinx students in preschool. It uses Foucault's lens of institutional power to describe policies and standards that impact each child's development through the Vygostskian lens. Furthermore, it uses the results to suggest developmentally and culturally effective strategies for the Latinx preschool classroom.

Raquel Plotka

One of my first assignments as a research assistant during the first few weeks of my doctoral training was to observe the development of self-regulation in Latinx toddlers. I had just moved from Argentina to begin my doctoral studies at Fordham University, and this was an emotional time for me. I had left behind friends and family with sad goodbyes at the airport, and New York City felt lonely and isolated. Ariella, my oldest, was then a toddler, learning to express herself through words, although most of the time she expressed herself through tantrums and crying. It was a difficult time for her too, as everything she knew had changed. She had left beloved grandparents and toys behind, and the only constant thing in her life was me.

My advisor was conducting a large research study with Latinx toddlers. She had hundreds of recorded observations of toddlers in a delayed gratification task. During the observations, toddlers were asked not to touch the "nice toy" and to play instead with a "plain toy." My job was to use a scoring rubric to decide whether the toddlers in the study had passed or failed the task; those who did not play with the "nice toy" had passed and were exhibiting the first signs of emotional regulation.

I spent days on campus observing toddlers being told not to touch the more fun toy until the researchers said so while coming home to my toddler daughter still struggling to master the skills of emotional regulation and self-control. After a few weeks of observing this struggle at home and in school, a few questions began to form in my head. Some of these questions have guided my work for the next decade and served as a guide for several of the issues explored in this book.

While observing the children struggling to wait to play with the more fun toy, I started asking myself the following: what about the children who waited 20 seconds and then touched the toy? Isn't that a sign of delayed gratification? What about the children who only waited five seconds? Isn't that more significant than just reaching out for the toy without any struggle at all? Having a toddler at home, I appreciated how long five seconds can feel when waiting for a favorite snack, toy, or person to come home. Other questions began to form themselves in my head as well: How come some children can wait longer than others? What are some things children "tell themselves" in their heads while waiting for the desired toy? Are some messages more effective than others? How much language do children need to master to be able to talk to themselves in that way?

At home and at work I was exposed to children developing language for the first time. Both the children in the research study and my daughter Ariella were learning Spanish as a first language, while growing up in a multilingual world. I then started wondering that, if emotional regulation is so tied to language skills, how does learning more than one language during early childhood affect this process?

I have just moved from my homeland to a new country 8,500 kilometers away. This part was obvious, yet I started realizing slowly that I have also moved from one culture to another equally distant one. Interactions were different here, and society followed new rules, dynamics, and meanings. People prioritized different things, and values were significantly dissimilar to those in my home country. I found myself at the intersection of two cultures with the task of socializing my young child. I was at the very beginning of the process of acculturation, adopting values and beliefs from my new culture while conserving the ideals of my homeland. My next research question was naturally forming: does culture shape the way we understand behavior? To what extent are developmental tasks such as emotional regulation shaped by culture? How does that play out in children who are growing up in multicultural contexts? Being an immigrant in a big city, I noticed that parenting is not an individual process, but at its core is a cultural practice. It is through parenting that we pass along our values and beliefs, and culture shapes child-rearing goals, objectives, and aspirations. I began wondering to what extent culture has an impact on adult practices that later shape a child's ability to regulate emotions.

At home, Ariella started adjusting to her new life and routines. Her behavior became more predictable and her emotions more regulated. I started asking myself what actions I had taken that helped her with this transition. While observing the children in the research study, I started paying attention to what language and behaviors parents used while trying to direct their children to comply with the instructions the researchers provided. I began asking questions such as: Is there a correlation between adult talk and behavior and children's ability to regulate emotions? Is compliance a behavioral manifestation of emotional regulation? What are the most helpful messages and actions adults can provide?

What I found was that the role of adults is central to children's ability to develop the ability to manage difficult emotions. Similarly, the early years are key to the development of these skills, and how adults interact with young children during these years have a lasting effect on children's lives. I asked myself once more, how do adults learn to help children develop self-regulatory skills? What information and training are necessary for adults in order to help young Latinx children gain self-regulatory skills in the context of multicultural and multilingual development?

These experiences and questions have guided the work presented in this book. I hope they help shape a generation of educators who appreciate the great struggle children experience when developing emotional regulation and are up to the challenge of helping young Latinx children reach this goal.

· 1 ·

EARLY CHILDHOOD PROGRAMS AND LATINX CHILDREN

Before discussing the association between self-regulation in Latinx children and existing early childhood programs, we need to begin with the state of our current educational system in order to better understand the impacts that current practices have on overall development. Self-regulation is the ability to control one's thoughts, emotions, and behaviors. However, it is a far more complex and multifaceted function that requires an in-depth analysis. Hence, chapter 2 and, specifically, chapter 3 will provide a detailed definition of and literature on self-regulation.

Because of the call for an increased focus on accountability and high-stakes testing, educational legislation has put the overall development of the preschool child at risk (Miller & Almon, 2009). Currently, educational practices rely on high-stakes testing and accountability without regard for core skills such as self-regulation and social competencies (Liew, 2012). Self-regulation can be briefly defined as the ability to control behavioral and emotional impulses and respond positively to others' cues. According to Bronson (2000), self-regulation is the core of being human, and "it underlies our assumptions about choice, decision making, and planning" (p. 1). Self-regulation involves emotions, behavioral, and cognitive self-regulation. Each area has distinct and overlapping processes. In this book, impulse control will be referenced to discuss emotional and behavioral. Policymakers are interested in seeing data from standardized tests and making educational decisions based on what these tests claim to measure. Equating the results of standardized test scores with actual learning, without considering or measuring for other cognitive and non-cognitive abilities in a child, is misleading.

Equating scores with knowledge adds an additional learning barrier for Latinx preschoolers. Research has suggested that Latinx students who speak English and Spanish and are characterized as Dual Language Learners (DLL) enter preschools with lower levels of self-regulatory abilities. DLLs are children who specifically range in age from 0 to 5 years old and are developing two languages at the same time. These children are also growing up in two distinct cultures (Castro et al., 2013). They are a different subgroup of bilingual students who typically have some social language and are developing social and academic language in a second language.

Why do Latinx preschoolers have lower levels of self-regulation? Many factors contribute to this crisis. The factors range from the lack of policies that explicitly address the characteristics and needs of Latinx preschoolers to the children's lack of access to preschool programs and curricula that support the needs of Latinx students. Focusing on just cognitive abilities without meeting the social and bicultural needs of the Latinx child is detrimental to their academic development.

Latinx preschoolers comprise 26% of children in the United States younger than five. While Latinx people make up one of the fastest-growing U.S. demographics, over 12 million Latinx families live below the poverty line (Ferjan Ramirez & Kuhl, 2017). This contributes to Latinx families living in communities with schools that are also economically challenged, which, in turn, affects the types of services and quality of education they receive from a young age. Attending schools that lack adequate resources also negatively affects all developmental domains during preschool. Latinx students living in struggling communities do not have the same access to early childhood programs as their peers in middle-class or affluent communities do. By the age of two, they are already falling behind academically and struggle socially and emotionally more than those who attend preschool programs with quality education. These struggles affect their respective levels of school readiness, which is a factor in executive functioning skills and, later, academic competence. Latinx preschoolers who attend schools considered to be economically disadvantaged tend to be more compliant and more reserved than other students and struggle more than Caucasian preschoolers with the development of impulse and cognitive control (McFadyen-Ketchum et al., 2016). Hence, these behaviors can reflect academic and socio-emotional challenges that result from living in poverty. Those Latinx preschoolers who are able to enroll in local preschool programs are often exposed to curricula that are neither culturally sensitive nor grounded in concepts of culturally responsive practices, which exacerbates the lack of support for self-regulation skills in Latinx preschoolers.

Preschool Curricula Today

In the past decade, and particularly in the early childhood research field, there has been much emphasis placed on the need to prepare students to be school-ready by addressing both academic and non-cognitive aspects of development. Non-cognitive aspects include socializing with peers, controlling personal emotions, and regulating one's own behaviors. Although preschools try to balance out both types of development, there is greater stress placed on supporting young learners' academic skills.

Today's kindergarten children are expected to be able to self-regulate their emotions and behaviors when entering school; specifically they are expected to internalize and follow set classroom rules and routines and to know a myriad of literacy and mathematical concepts. Miller and Almon (2009) report that 76% of New York City kindergarten teachers spend more than one hour of their classroom time on literacy instruction, 26% spend more than one hour on math, and about 79% report spending time on test preparation. Based on this data, it is important that young children attend a preschool that prepares them to meet the rigorous academic standards they will encounter in a formal school setting.

Furthermore, while some preschool programs have included executive functioning concepts, those programs do not typically foster the specific cultural needs of Latinx preschoolers. Some preschool curricula that embed self-regulatory skills in their preschool classrooms today are as follows: (a) Promoting Alternative Thinking Strategies, (b) Creative Curriculum, (c) Tools of the Mind, Chicago School Readiness Project (CSRP), and (d) Head Start Research-Based Developmentally Informed (REDI).

Promoting Alternative Thinking Strategies (PATHS)

Promoting Alternative Thinking Strategies (PATHS) is a socio-emotional-oriented curriculum in preschool that aims to improve children's emotional knowledge, self-regulation, and social skills. The researchers suggest PATHS as a curriculum for preschool programs that is intended to prevent or reduce behavioral and emotional problems in young children as well as enhance children's social and emotional competence (Domitrovich et al., 2007, p. 70). This program uses a neurocognitive developmental approach that provides young children with specific strategies to control themselves and understand their emotions.

Creative Curriculum

Similar to the PATHS program is the Creative Curriculum. It is a preschool curriculum that is primarily focused on providing a socio-emotional-based experience in learning. The Creative Curriculum allows for social interaction opportunities for preschool children to develop and acquire new skills. It is also based on the principle that preschool curricula needs to address social competence and do more than just place an emphasis on academics. The founders of the curriculum suggest that social, emotional, and physical areas of development can be integrated in order to achieve gains in cognitive skills. This curriculum also considers the physical environment of the child to be as important as the role of the educator in promoting learning.

Tools of the Mind (TOM)

Programs such as Tools of the Mind (TOM) have self-regulatory activities as the foundation of any learning activity that takes place in the classroom (Bodrova & Leong, 2008). TOM's core activity revolves around the concept of play and having the children plan for play. Self-regulatory skills can best be developed through the use of social interactions with peers, games, and, most importantly, play. The TOM curriculum also has been used in preschools as an intervention to help children develop self-regulatory skills. The focus of the program is on symbolic play, which is said to promote self-regulation. This curriculum facilitates the development of these skills in a systematic way, including in its emotional, social, and cognitive aspects. TOM addresses self-regulatory skills through different activities throughout the day.

The Chicago School Readiness Project (CSRP)

Research concludes that interventions in the preschool years could prevent academic delays and can also eliminate the potential for students to become considered "at-risk." The Chicago School Readiness Project (CSRP; Raver et al., 2011) is a classroom intervention that provides an assessment of low-income preschoolers' emotional and behavioral self-regulation. The CSRP implemented self-regulation measures from the Preschool Self-Regulation Assessment (PSRA), which captured children's behavioral, impulse, and attention control, as well as executive functioning skills. CSRP specifically focuses on incorporating training and support for educators to efficiently stop recurrent episodes of misbehavior in children by setting clear rules, regulations, and routines.

Head Start Research-Based, Developmentally Informed (REDI)

Similar to the PATHS program is the *Head Start Research-Based, Developmentally Informed (REDI)* intervention, a research-based practice for teachers to support the development of self-regulatory skills (Bierman et al., 2008). REDI involves classroom lessons that are implemented with follow-up activities after each lesson. These lessons and activities are extended to the home setting in an effort to improve children's school readiness in literacy and language. Teachers in the program teach explicit lessons on social and emotional skills while mentoring the students. The teachers in the study encouraged the use of emotional coaching, induction strategies, and problem-solving techniques throughout the day to support preschool children's development of social-emotional skills. The program is integrated into existing preschool programs, such as *High/Scope* and *Creative Curriculum*.

The programs mentioned above focus on developing self-regulatory skills, but each lacks the aspects that are most valued by the Latinx community in supporting their children at school. Specifically, they do not embed the critical aspects of *familismo*, *respeto*, and *educación*.

What Are *Familismo, Respeto,* and *Educación*?

The Latinx community is an inclusive and diverse culture, one that encompasses dialects of Spanish and Indigenous native languages. Religious, spiritual beliefs, and practices also vary. Yet, while each culture has its own norms, there are three cultural values that are at the core of the Latinx community: *familismo, respeto,* and *educación. Familismo, respeto,* and *educación* are values used as parenting goals. Latinx families' perceptions of self-regulation—specifically, their views on the development of self-regulation in relation to the family or the group that surrounds the child, rather than as an individual skill that children develop on their own—is different in significant ways from those of the dominant U.S. culture.

Familismo refers to the value of maintaining close family ties and includes the expectation that the family should be the primary source of emotional and instrumental support, with loyalty and commitment to the family taking precedence over individual needs and desires (Fracasso & Busch-Rossnagel, 1992). It is important to understand that the term *familismo* includes the notion that problems, issues, and concerns should be resolved within the family, and that outsiders should not be included in decisions related to a family member's well-being, social and emotional development, or psychological state. This value can have implications for the way Latinx families interact with and understand educators' efforts to make recommendations or assist in realms such as a child's social development, happiness, and well-being, which are, in Latinx culture, traditionally assumed to belong to the family. *Familismo* might also affect a family's willingness to seek outside help to deal with learning or other disabilities.

Respeto refers to the maintenance of harmonious interpersonal relationships through respect for others, which includes respecting the roles of each person in the family. From a young age, children are taught to greet elders politely, not to challenge an elder's point of view, and not to interrupt an adult's conversation (Fracasso & Busch-Rossnagel, 1992). Similarly, the value of *respeto* proposes to treat professionals and experts with deference. Traditionally, Latinxs treat teachers and educators with great respect and might find it disrespectful to act as equal partners with them, share with them the power of decision-making, or make suggestions to them related to curriculum or program services. Latinx parents are often apprehensive of questioning a school's authority, as it goes against their belief systems regarding authority and respect (Smith, Stern, & Shatrova, 2008). Similarly, parents might feel it is inappropriate to ask questions and might defer to the educators when it comes to their children's education. This attitude can interfere with the American definition of "engagement" and thus make Latinx families look disengaged. Parental engagement refers to the participation of significant caregivers, such as parents, grandparents, stepparents, foster parents, etc., in the development of the education process of their children; it encompasses activities that take place in the home, early education program, and within the community. The most widely cited definition is Epstein's typology, which includes six components: (a) parenting, including providing basic needs and emotional support; (b) communication with educators; (c) supporting learning at home, such as reading or helping with homework; (d) attending school/center events; (e) participating in community connections, such as a parent collaborating with community institutions and agencies to facilitate development and learning; and (f) decision-making and parent participation in center or school governance (Epstein et al., 1996).

Likewise, this respect and authority are considered a two-way system between parents and the school. Parents expect educators to respect their child-rearing decisions, and questioning parental involvement can be perceived as a critique and often as disrespectful (Delgado-Gaitan, 2004). Latinx families value the education of the whole child. The word *educación* in Spanish, however, has a broader meaning than "education" in English. *Educación* includes not only academic development but also involves the development of social skills, self-regulation, compliance, respect, patience, and delayed gratification. The current educational climate might ignore an essential part of early childhood education that is highly cherished by Latinx families. The central role that self-regulation plays in early childhood development and education has prompted academics and educators to question current curricula, especially when it comes to teaching and learning for Latinx children, and in engaging families.

The Growing Gap of Self-Regulatory Skills in Latinx Preschoolers

The lack of policies and access to quality early childhood programs that support Latinx young learners puts them at a greater academic disadvantage than that faced by their Caucasian peers. Broadening the crisis is the fact that young learners who enter kindergarten without self-regulatory skills are at greater risk for difficulties such as peer rejection and low levels of academic achievement than those who do have those skills when they start school. Research suggests that lower academic achievement can be attributed to the decrease in self-regulatory abilities of preschool children. Regulatory skills are related to academic achievement, school readiness, and future success. These skills require guidance in developing and applying them for problem-solving strategies in classrooms. Over time, "the developmental increases reflect advances in an underlying cognitive ability to represent complex rule structures such as those contained in response inhibition" (Blair & Razza, 2007, p. 652). Therefore, these regulatory skills are essential in preschool classrooms and in subsequent elementary school years.

When early childhood programs are guided by a system that emphasizes test-driven curricula resulting from current educational policies, Latinx preschoolers face significant academic challenges that do not address their needs (Castro et al., 2013). Latinx preschoolers need to have programs that address non-cognitive aspects of development while skillfully supporting academics such as literacy and language development. This is the case because language is a key factor in the ability to self-regulate, which then leads to academic gains. Moreover, Latinx preschoolers were shown to develop regulatory skills at a slower rate than English-language proficient preschoolers.

The relationship and interactions between the two languages have many advantages in children's overall development, particularly in executive function. Nonetheless, there is a paucity of literature that specifically examines the associations between Latinx preschoolers and self-regulation skills. While this topic is one that has been extensively researched regarding Caucasian preschoolers, the study of these associations in Latinx students who speak Spanish and English and live in bicultural homes is lacking. As the Latinx population continues to grow, it is imperative to examine the relationship between language and self-regulation among Latinx preschoolers for application to policy and curriculum development (Castro et al., 2013). Viewing current educational policy through Foucault's framework, as will be done in the next chapter, it is apparent that educational power is being taken away from classroom teachers and given to lawmakers and administrators, who are focusing solely on academics.

Summary

This chapter reviewed the limited research that looks at the development of self-regulatory skills in Latinx children. It also summarized typical early childhood curricula and the alarming concern in the lack of practices that foster these skills in Latinx students. The next chapter introduces the theoretical framework that will guide the focus of this book.

· 2 ·

THEORETICAL BACKGROUND: FOUCAULT AND VYGOTSKY

Chapter 1 introduced the statement of the problem, whereas this chapter will provide key perspectives from the Vygotskian and Foucaultian frameworks that guided this study and provide a review of the research and literature related to the development of self-regulation in early childhood education.

To better understand the factors that influence the development of self-regulation in Latinx students, it is key to evaluate the state of the early childhood field. Questioning current approaches and standards can allow for the development of different perspectives within the field of early childhood education. Examining the interactions between standards, policies, early childhood programs, as well as pedagogy, is critical. These aspects function as a system that directly impacts the individual development of young learners (see Figure 1). Specifically, policies and standards have a trickle-down effect on each child's development. Two frameworks will be used to examine these issues. First, Foucault's post-structural theory states that a set of governed systems shapes society. From Foucault's perspective, an educational institution can be described as a set structure that exercises power over the knowledge taught to the preschool child and describes the influence these institutions have as the active link between the family and the workforce. These set structures affect the workforce of early childhood educators. An impact on young

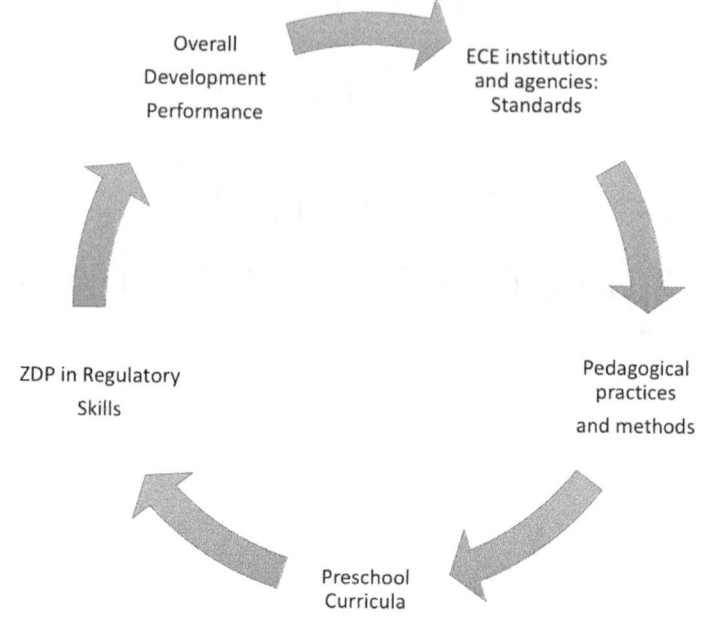

Figure 1. Power/Influences and Self-Regulation in Early Childhood

learners is also observed, specifically as it relates to their individual development, or, as the Vygotskian perspective (the second framework) suggests, their Zone of Personal Development (ZPD). Through these lenses, the effects of institutional power can be described—particularly that power's influence on the several roles involved in the development of executive functions, such as self-regulation, that revolve around language. Language is a core foundation for Latinx students who grow up in bilingual communities.

Analyzing the current early childhood education system through a Foucaultian lens of power, in which state standards and legislation mandate the implementation of specific pedagogical practices, shows the effects/impacts of self-regulatory skills on developments delineated by Vygotsky.

Institutional Power

Foucault (1980) categorized power through the development of disciplinary power and described institutional power within disciplinary power. Discipline is a mechanism of power that is used to observe and regulate behavior and "aims to target the individual involved in groups and institutions" (Murray-Chandler, 2009, p. 55). Foucault also states that discipline is a one-way power exercised in an organization or institution: "Discipline 'makes' individuals; it is a specific technique of a power that regards individuals both as objects and as instruments of its exercise" (1980, p. 170). Foucault suggested that those who do not stay within the limits established by the institution are "isolated, labeled delinquent and are sometimes used to demonstrate to others what happens when one doesn't follow the way of that particular school" (Murray-Chandler, 2009, p. 58).

If we look at the early childhood education system, we can see an example of the exercise of institutional power as disciplinary power. The National Association for the Education of Young Children (NAEYC) has written guidelines on Developmentally Appropriate Practice (DAP) for educators and administrators to follow. Those preschools that follow the DAP standards can receive accreditation for their programs, which leads the preschool to be "equated with program quality" (Cohen, 2008, p. 17). The rigorous process of becoming NAEYC accredited involves the meeting of staff, administrators, and educational program qualifications, as well as on-site visits. These regulations establish the institutional power that state and local agencies have over the curriculum and practice of early childhood education through knowledge that has been developed and adopted as norms in the education field. Sanctions such as receiving demerits lead administrators and teachers to focus on compliance with the rules set under the institutional power that schools hold. The need of the preschool child is no longer the main focus. Instead, the academic achievement standards set by institutions such as the NAEYC, written discourses such as the DAP, and educational policies such as Race to the Top are seen in the monitoring of daily activities for the preschool child. Focus on preschool self-regulatory skills, which lead to cognitive development, is put at risk when the power possessed by early childhood education agencies is solely aimed at the introduction of literacy and numeracy as the only form of cognitive development early on.

"Regimes of Truth"

Michel Foucault defines "regimes of truth" as a mechanism that produces discourse, rules, and/or regulations, which then function as true in a particular field:

> "Truth" is to be understood as a system of ordered procedures for the production, regulation, distribution, circulation and operation of statements. "Truth" is linked in a circular relation with systems of power which produce and sustain it, and to effects of power which it induces and which extend it. A "regime" of truth. (1980, p. 133)

In the Foucaultian framework, truths regarding the development of the preschool child exist in education in order to regulate appropriate pedagogical practices. The academic pressure placed on the higher school grades has "trickled down even to young children, with a growing number of mandates imposed on early education programs to be responsible for young children's academic readiness and learning" (p. 766). Additionally, Nadeem et al. (2010) state that "the prominent emphasis placed on academic achievement, when juxtaposed with the abundant scientific literature on the importance of social and emotional competencies for the long-term success of young children, suggests that some current educational policies may be misaligned" (p. 766). Nadeem et al. (2010) concur with the findings of Miller and Almon (2009) that "long-term research casts doubts on the assumption that starting earlier on the teaching of phonics and other discrete skills leads to better results" (p. 7). Diamond et al. (2007) report that educators are under time limitations and constraints, allowing for focus on just instruction in classrooms. Yet, the regime of truth established by governmental entities and carried out by state and local agencies focuses on academics, not on curricula focusing on self-regulatory development as the appropriate teaching apparatus in early childhood. It is this relationship between knowledge and power, which will be further analyzed in the next section, that governs the early childhood education field.

Knowledge and Power

"Truth is centered on the form of scientific discourse and the institutions which produce it" (Foucault, 1980, p. 131). Foucault believes that mechanisms of power produce knowledge. That knowledge is then used to compel humans to follow it and to subject themselves to the knowledge collected and established as truth in the given field. In Foucaultian terms and in relation to early childhood education, today's pedagogical practices focus on non-play methods of fostering cognitive development in the preschool child, as those methods are thought of as truth or knowledge in the field. School reform initiatives are driven by scientific research, such as state-mandated testing written into the

Race to the Top and Common Core State Standards (CCSS). It is the ideology of educating the child to test well that has led to the introduction of academics at the preschool level and the resulting neglect in focusing on young children's development of self-regulation. This "knowledge" that literacy and numeracy are the best things for preschoolers to learn has been established as "truth" through the use of power exercised by government and educational agencies that produced that very knowledge.

The consequence of these truths imposed on the education of the preschool child through the current pedagogical methods is the lack of self-regulatory development, which can negatively influence academic skills. The results from this study were used to provide and support new truths regarding the associations between self-regulation and academics in early childhood. Since these results support a different regime of power/knowledge, there could emerge the implementation of curricula capable of sustaining the development of critical aspects such as self-regulation as supported by the Vygotskian framework.

Socialization in the Early Years

The Vygotskian framework, named after its formulator, Lev Vygotsky, suggests that the construction of knowledge is mediated by the social and cultural interactions of the preschool child. Prosocial behaviors are associated with cognitive maturation, specifically language. Additionally, these behaviors can also support early stages of literacy, such as the ability to listen and communicate, which are the main components learned in all social settings. In the preschool setting, programs that include a social component can assist in addressing the academic achievements of students. In general, preschool children who lack social skills also have developmental problems in self-control, emotional regulation, and school readiness (Arslan et al., 2011). More generally, children's ability to regulate emotions and behaviors is positively related to school readiness. In young learners, there are direct links between social competence, expressive language, and pre-literacy skills.

With respect to the Latinx population, socialization becomes a critical component in development. Latinx preschoolers are not just learning language but are also learning to be part of a different cultural group. Integration of Latinx preschoolers into social settings reduces risks for social and language problems. Socialization also allows for language development, as it takes at least three to seven years for Latinx preschoolers to develop English language proficiency in school settings. Castro et al. (2013) and Luchtel et al. (2010) reveal that socialization can further support academic achievement in Latinx students. Chang et al. (2007) propose that the bonds and interactions established through socialization can facilitate changes in self-confidence and identity. Social interactions can ultimately increase opportunities for more academic learning in preschool children.

Zone of Proximal Development (ZPD)

Vygotsky describes the Zone of Proximal Development (ZPD) as the difference between a child's actual developmental level and the tasks that he/she can reach with the assistance of adults and more mature peers. Preschool children can achieve their ZPD by receiving feedback from their peers and adults that helps them understand sociocultural and historical expectations. Vygotsky indicated that a child could only reach their ZPD through modeling and then imitating behaviors that are within their developmental level. Adults can ensure that the child can remain within their ZPD while developing higher-level executive functions, including self-regulation. Vygotsky also attributed the development of preschoolers' ZPD to self-regulation through forms of language.

Language

Language is thought to be the link between the individual and the individual's environment. Language learning is an important marker of knowledge about affect regulation. Vygotsky (1978) describes private speech as speech that "originates from the social world of the child in children's interactions with others ... which function in part to guide and regulate children's attention and behavior" (Winsler et al., 2009, p. 4). Specifically, it is "children's private, or self-directed, speech as the primary means for transferring regulation of behavior from others to self and as the fundamental tool for self-guidance and self-direction" (Elias & Berk 2002, p. 218). Language in the early years plays a distinct role, specifically, the role of private speech in the development of self-regulatory skills. In Latinx preschoolers, the impact of language on executive functions such as self-regulation becomes critical for academic development. Language proficiency in Latinx preschoolers can allow for greater abilities in inhibitory control, executive functions, and self-regulation (Castro et al., 2013; McClelland et al., 2007; Winsler et al., 2009). There is a relationship between the level of proficiency in language acquisition that a child achieves and that child's self-efficacy skills. This relationship is a unique one for the Latinx child who is developing two languages simultaneously.

Vygotsky stresses the significant role of "inner speech and verbal self-instructions in self-control" (Gruber & Goschke, 2004, p. 112) and says that the central component of advanced preparation involves the retrieval of a verbal task or goal representation into working memory. Self-regulation begins when children control their behavior through private speech that assimilates prompts, demands, and explanations from adults (Elias & Berk, 2002). Elias and Berk (2002) describe how children use "language to control such complex cognitive processes as attention, memory, planning, and self-reflection ... eventually, private speech is internalized as inner verbal thought" (p. 218). Words that are internalized by the child become mental tools that are then manipulated to regulate behavior. Language is the first mental tool acquired, as it gives way to the acquisition of other needed mental tools in the development of self-regulation.

Specifically, language is used as a regulatory function during moments of emotional frustration and to express needs and wants. Day and Smith (2013) describe their methods as "examining children's private speech aids in understanding how children regulate emotion" (p. 410). Their results imply that language interacts with strategies of emotional regulation. Thus, language developments have an association with regulatory development.

Summary

Although the theories of Foucault and Vygotsky are vastly different, it is Foucault's description of the structures of society and the form in which Vygotsky describes learning for the preschool child that binds the two theories together. Foucault's description of power can be applied to early childhood education in globalized terms, while Vygotsky focuses on a smaller branch of early childhood education, specifically describing ZPD in self-regulation. The ideology of power is seen in the regimes of power in education that trickle down and impact the ZPD of self-regulatory skills through forced academic-only preschool curricula. The following chapter will explore different types of self-regulation and the critical associations for Latinx children.

· 3 ·

SELF-REGULATION AND CRITICAL ASSOCIATIONS

The previous chapter provided key perspectives from the Vygotskian and Foucaultian frameworks that provided a foundation for the effects that the lack of self-regulation can have on Latinx children. It also summarized the current curricula and how it plays a role in the way these skills are taught today. This chapter will describe what self-regulation is and how it is associated with many critical aspects of education in young children.

Miller and Almon (2009) state, "extremely chaotic classrooms and extremely teacher-directed classrooms are counterproductive to the development of self-regulation and other underlying skills in children" (p. 22). The lack of focus on self-regulatory skills was viewed through Foucault's perspective of power. Current educational policies were described as having power and, thus, regulating preschool curricula through state learning standards. The goal of this research was to investigate the development of self-regulatory skills in preschool children in an urban school district. Self-regulation is best taught by allowing children opportunities to socialize in which they practice the rules of certain behaviors and apply those rules to new situations. As discussed in the previous chapter, the Vygotskian framework also defines associations between the development of regulatory skills and instruction and academic development.

Self-Regulation

Self-regulation "is a deep, internal mechanism that enables children as well as adults to engage in mindful, intentional, and thoughtful behaviors" (Bodrova & Leong, 2008, p. 56). Vygotsky's theories on speech stated that self-regulation is the internalizing process of a caregiver's regulatory speech to a child. The ability to control emotions and behaviors enables a student to perform well on tasks. By contrast, the lack of development of self-regulatory skills affects cognitive skills, since students without these skills are not able to sufficiently self-regulate their own learning, leading to poor academic performance.

Bronson (2000) states that the lack of preschool socialization has not only cognitive and emotional effects during the early years; there are also neurological and biological consequences: "Brain developments, especially in the frontal lobes, support the child's growing cognitive control of attention, working memory, and problem solving" (2000, p. 162). The ability to direct behavior and self-regulate is associated with frontal cortex function and is linked to educational attainment (Spinella & Miley, 2004). The ability to use abstract thought and regulate cognition takes place in the frontal cortex, and the classroom environment of the preschool child becomes critical in the development of the cortex. An early childhood classroom environment plays an important role in the development of (a) the frontal cortex and (b) the brain's neural connections and executive control systems in the frontal lobe. It is important that children are provided with stimulating classroom environments and numerous social interactions. This is why the presented study investigated the development of self-regulation and academics in students attending preschool programs with the use of a reliable measurement instrument for field-based research.

Self-regulation is best taught to young children by allowing them creative opportunities to practice the rules of certain behaviors and apply those rules to new situations. Based on the Vygotskian perspective, the ability to act intentionally involves the internalization of higher mental functions that develop through social relations between parent/caregiver and child, teacher and child, or older peers and child. Self-regulation has also been defined as having two major factors. The first refers to the capacity to monitor inhibitory aspects. Inhibitory control refers to the ability to suppress impulsive thoughts or behavior and resist surrounding temptations and additional distractions. The second factor is working memory, which is the ability of a child to hold, update, and manipulate verbal and nonverbal information. Self-regulatory skills represent an important developmental factor in young children, as such skills allow them control over their thoughts, feelings, and behavior.

In a classroom setting, a child shows his or her ability to self-regulate when that child stops doing what he/she is engaged in when a teacher says to stop. This can extend to an academic context because children's level of self-regulatory skills correlates to the level of attention given to math and literacy concepts in school. Research suggests that the development of self-regulation allows children to later self-regulate their learning, impacting their academic performance in a school setting (Bronson, 2000; Tominey & McClelland, 2011; Winsler et al., 2009).

Kindergarten educators view the ability of incoming students to follow and carry out directions and the ability to socially interact as a better indicator than academic skills of school readiness (Lin et al., 2003). Specifically, kindergarten educators believe both the ability to be non-disruptive and the ability to communicate are essential, particularly as compared to their ability to count to 20 or more, or know the alphabet, names, colors, shapes, and motor skills (Lin et al., 2003).

There are several types of self-regulation skills that are developed in early childhood: behavioral and emotional regulation, as well as cognitive regulation. Self-regulation will be discussed in the context of the overall impact it has on child development, explicitly on language, social skills, and effects on academics. The following sections will focus on the development of (a) behavioral, emotional, and cognitive regulation, (b) self-regulation and language, (c) self-regulation and social skills, (d) academic achievement, (e) self-regulation and emergent literacy skills, and (f) Latinx preschoolers.

Behavioral, Emotional, and Cognitive Regulation

Cognitive regulation is the capacity to do something because it is needed and to have the ability to think ahead to possible consequences. Cognitive regulation is also the ability to consider more appropriate and alternative forms of action. Hence, when young learners transition to elementary school with both disruptive behavioral and emotional problems, they are at a greater risk of dropping out of school. This study suggests that inattention and aggression predicted high school dropout rates more than socioeconomic status and other family factors. Therefore, teaching children how to regulate themselves behaviorally and emotionally is crucial to academic development.

In preschool, teachers expect children to be able to monitor their emotions and their behavior according to what is accepted as proper in the classroom setting (Bronson, 2000). Appropriate behavior is the ability to "delay, defer, and accept substitutions without becoming aggressive or disorganized by frustration" (Bronson, 2000, p. 71). Murray and Kochanska (2002) suggest that levels of self-regulation are correlated to the frequency of maladaptive behaviors and problematic temperaments in early childhood. Their longitudinal study explored the development and structure of self-regulation at different stages ranging from toddlerhood to early school age. The four-year study assessed (a) the ability to delay children's impulses using snacks and toys, (b) fine or gross motor movement through finger movements as well as walking slowly on a line set on the floor, and (c) stopping ongoing responses from children by relaying alternate responses through commands given by play puppets, asking for different responses and behaviors from children (Murray & Kochanska, 2002).

Similarly, Smith-Donald et al. (2007) measured emotional and behavioral self-regulation skills using the Preschool Self-Regulation Assessment (PSRA). The PSRA is a battery of self-regulatory tasks that were adapted from Murray and Kochanska's (2002) effortful control tasks and executive control tasks. For the executive control tasks, the PSRA also adapted a task from the Diamond and Taylor (1996) tapping test. The tapping task was administered to young children and required the child to remember two rules: when the researcher taps once, the subject is to tap twice, and vice versa. The researchers concluded that the test required the children (from 3.5-year-olds to 7-year-olds) to remember two rules and the ability to inhibit response tendencies. The results of the tapping test imply that these abilities improved between the ages of 3 and 7, which correlates to changes in the frontal cortex. Smith-Donald et al. (2007) concluded that there were correlations between self-regulation skills and social competence, behavior problems, and early academic skills based on their measures. The measures used were the PSRA and an assessor report based on children's emotions, attention, and behavior during evaluations. Concurrent with these self-regulation measures, the Peabody Vocabulary Test (PPVT-III) and teachers' evaluation forms on behavior were collected and analyzed. Correspondingly, Denham et al. (2012b) tested 392 Head Start and private child-care center students also utilizing the PSRA assessments and found that self-regulation skills predicted learning behaviors in the classroom.

The ability to modify one's behavior impacts the academic gains of a child, as suggested by Tominey and McClelland (2011). They examined 65 preschool children during circle time games and found that children who had better self-regulatory skills also had better word-letter recognition. The games used in the study were intended to help students with attention, working memory, and their overall inhibitory control. Findings suggest that circle time games that were presented to the children did in fact support significant gains in behavioral self-regulatory skills. Although emotional and behavioral regulation are two different forms of regulation, they are often described under one category, as previously mentioned. However, growth in both types of self-regulation skills was evident in preschool children who had been exposed to circle time games.

Behavioral regulation in preschool children enables them to consciously comply with adult directions and instructions and modify their behavior. Behavioral regulation contributes to self-control in classrooms, which is associated with levels of school readiness. Specifically, when a child can follow directions and instructions, they are more likely to have the opportunity to focus and perform better in a school setting.

Denham et al. (2012a) observed the emotional knowledge, emotional and social behaviors, social problem-solving, and self-regulation of 275 preschool children and what affects children's motivation to learn, participate in the classroom, and other measures of academic success; they define emotional regulation as (a) the ability to control one's emotions in productive ways, (b) an awareness of feelings of proper and acceptable forms of emotion within varying situations, and (c) the ability to modify emotions. Emotional regulation is also described as the "ability and disposition to use and integrate social-emotional knowledge, regulatory abilities, empathy, perspective taking, and social skills in a seamless manner that is appropriate for the child within a given social context" (Nadeem et al., 2010, p. 767).

The ability to control one's emotional and behavioral state is a critical developing component for the preschool child. It is suggested that between the third and fourth years of a child's life, there are major developments in social and emotional understanding (Cole et al., 2009). Cole et al. (2009) describe this component as the socio-emotional competence and adjustment that makes considerable advances during the preschool years. As such, it is important to teach children to emotionally regulate through specific strategies that will reduce the level of distraction and will teach students to verbalize problems instead of crying or displaying disruptive behavior.

The ability to regulate emotions effectively is also linked to language skills, perhaps because more proficient language abilities allow children to better understand, modify, and cope with emotions (Cole et al., 2009). As previously mentioned, private speech in children can help with functions of emotional regulation. Therefore, the relationship between self-regulation and language in preschool children will be discussed now.

Self-Regulation and Language

As was discussed more generally at the end of the last chapter, much research has found links between language and self-regulation. The Vygotskian framework proposed that the concept of language in a child serves as a tool for the development of that child's self-regulation. Through the Vygostskian perspective, private speech originates from the child's interaction with their social world, and thus social speech between child and caregiver serves as a guide to regulate behavior and attention. Children communicate with adults and older peers and observe their actions/behaviors in order to regulate their own behaviors through the use of communication with oneself, or what Vygotsky called "private speech." The process of private speech becomes internalized as inner verbal thoughts, which leads to the ability to then self-regulate cognitive processes and direct and control one's behavior. Moreover, private speech not only has associations with cognitive regulation but it also explicitly allows young children the ability to regulate their emotions.

Using the Vygotskian framework, language is a mediating variable between functions of cognitive regulation. One example of this is when preschool children verbally instruct themselves on how to properly carry out an activity based on previous adult or older peer instruction. Receiving instructions from adults or peers contributes to the development of self-control, as this is closely related to receptive vocabulary in children. Perner, Lang, and Kloo (2002) also suggest that there is a strong association between receptive language and cognitive regulation. Receiving and modifying behavior through inner speech are the initial steps in the development of self-regulatory skills. According to Gruber and Goschke (2004), regulatory skills emerge from a dynamic interaction between the prefrontal-parietal and prefrontal-temporal cortical networks, which mediate attention, and the left hemispheric premotor and parietal brain regions, which mediate language. These verbal instructions become inner thoughts, allowing children to direct attention and behavior only through thoughts. It is here where self-regulatory skills acquire a deeper meaning.

Self-Regulation and Social Skills

Socialization and the use and development of social skills are the core elements that are evolving in the preschool child. This is one key domain that rapidly develops during early childhood. Once preschool children have developed emotionally and behaviorally, the ability to achieve social competence and peer acceptance emerge. A child who cannot control their behavior will experience negative and very little peer interaction. Hence, social competence has been linked to school readiness in preschool students. A child in the preschool years learns acceptable socialization skills through peer interactions and play. Through socialization, children will learn to modify and mold behaviors based on feedback received from their peers. Children learn how to inhibit disruptive and aggressive behaviors while forming friendships and establishing their roles in social contexts.

Other children will point out inappropriate behaviors, and those children may choose not to engage in play with the child who has not learned to regulate their behaviors. This feedback to the disruptive child is crucial since it can result in a change toward socially acceptable behavior. Denham et al. (2012b) state that the preschool child is socially competent when they are aware of, understand, and empathize with the feelings of their peers, and appreciate the similarities and differences of other children. Therefore, children must first develop an understanding of their behaviors and emotions so that they then can learn how to guide or regulate them in order to be socially accepted by peers.

Regulating emotional reactions is a vital skill that allows for integration into social contexts and/or social environments. Therefore, the lack of self-regulatory skills is linked to behavioral problems in preschool children. Children with a low level of self-regulation tend to deal poorly with change and have higher levels of anxiety and stress. By contrast, children with behavioral self-regulation can determine what is considered important and what needs their immediate attention in a classroom setting. They can focus on classroom tasks and/or adult instructions, despite being exposed to multiple stimuli, and can choose not to behave in a disruptive manner or engage/focus on other classroom distractions (Wanless et al., 2011).

Emotionality may be particularly relevant to the development of the cortex area of the brain, which conducts cognitive processes such as self-regulated learning (Blair, 2002). Thus, emotion and cognition need to be integrated to allow for regulatory skills to develop and for a child to show school progress. Maladaptive behaviors in young children will worsen if not targeted by educators in the early school years. These behaviors will prevent a child from undergoing healthy social development, consequently affecting academic achievements (Bierman et al., 2008). Self-regulatory skills have underlying developments that affect the academic outcomes of a child in later years. These skills begin to form/develop well before formal education takes place in the life of a young child. Therefore, allowing the opportunity for these skills to properly expand is a basis for age-appropriate emotional and behavioral growth.

As previously stated, focusing on regulating the emotional and social aspects of a child while embedding the cognitive aspect can lead to student academic gain.

Self-Regulation and Academic Achievement

Preschool students who lack strong behavioral self-regulation skills have difficulty performing in classrooms with set curricula and agendas (Blair, 2002; McClelland et al., 2007; Raver et al., 2011). Children with low levels of inhibitory control have difficulty paying attention in class. Impulsive behavior limits their ability to hold on to new information taught in classrooms and leads them to become unsuccessful students when tested in a formal school setting. Improving self-regulatory skills in young children can improve not only their overall development but numeracy and literacy development as well. Also, the development of these skills can potentially reduce the number of referrals given to children for special education, as well as suspensions, and thus improve retention in schools.

In addition, children's ability to regulate attention is important for cognitive competence (Garner & Waajid, 2012). Specifically, children's behavioral self-regulation has been found to predict their work habits (Rimm-Kaufman et al., 2009) and their ability to benefit from independent learning activities. Moreover, self-regulation emerges as a predictor of children's academic achievement as early as preschool (Blair & Razza, 2007; Denham et al., 2012b; McClelland et al., 2007). Early behavioral self-regulation has also been found to predict academic achievement in kindergarten and throughout elementary school (Liew et al., 2008; McClelland et al., 2006), and even high school and college completion (Vitaro et al., 2005). Willoughby et al. (2011) relate two types of regulation to distinct skills in preschool children: impulse control is related to inattentive-overactive behavior, while cognitive regulation relates to academic achievement.

Children who are able to control impulses in preschool demonstrate a better rate of adjustment to the school setting when entering elementary grades (Smith-Donald et al., 2007). Children who regulated better were reported to be more obedient, showed social competence, were more organized, and had effective task execution. Denham et al.'s research (2012a) suggests that, when assessed in kindergarten, preschool children who lack social-emotional regulatory skills were found to demonstrate less general knowledge acquisition, mathematical, language, and literacy skills than their peers with those skills. Teachers report, however, that there is high variability in the self-regulatory skills of children entering kindergarten (Lin et al., 2003).

Self-Regulation and Emergent Literacy Skills

Language and literacy are the main focus of young children's experiences. Language allows for communication, leading the child to greater opportunities for learning and continuous development. Print concepts and alphabet skills, along with early literacy skills, can be developed through the use of dramatic play, games, storybooks, and language experiences.

As a result of the great importance of language and literacy, detecting difficulties in reading during the preschool years is vital for literacy development in the upper grades (Farver et al., 2007). Molfese et al. (2006) examined reading skills in preschool students to determine the development of skills in non-reading preschool children. They specifically defined what is entailed in literacy skills and conducted a correlational analysis to measure the association between literacy and language. The main factors considered important in measuring and comparing gains in letter identification among preschool students, according to Molfese et al. (2006), are as follows: (a) phonological processing, (b) rhyming, (c) print knowledge, and (d) scores on *Get Ready to Read* (GRTR). The authors found a correlation between letter identification and the above factors. However, the study authors also note that age and general cognitive skills may have influenced children's performance on tests (Molfese et al., 2006). Nonetheless, literacy skills are defined not just by print concepts but also by phonological awareness and vocabulary skills. Addressing literacy skills is vital to academic achievement, but assessing children with proper measures, either in Spanish or English, is needed to prevent students from falling behind in literacy development (Farver et al., 2007). The section below will review the studies that discuss literacy skills as defined above and their relationship to self-regulation.

Self-regulation contributes to literacy achievement in early grade-school years. Liew et al. (2008) conducted a longitudinal study looking at self-regulation and academics. The researchers tested 733 students entering first grades in literacy, math, and measures of regulation. The students were tested on a yearly basis until the completion of the third year. The results specifically revealed that scores in first-grade self-regulation measures predicted literacy development in the third grade. Similarly, Ursache, Blair, and Raver (2012) conducted a study in which preschool curricula were evaluated in terms of self-regulation and academic development. They focused on three preschool programs, all of which were briefly explained in Chapter 1—Head Start Research-Based Developmentally Informed (REDI), Tools of the Mind (TOM), and Chicago School Readiness Project (CSRP)—and their effects on literacy measures. The researchers suggest that classrooms that practice self-regulation skills have a large impact on overall academic achievements.

A different study, by McClelland et al. (2007), consisted of a battery of assessments administered to English and Spanish-speaking preschoolers. It included background questionnaires, a behavior regulation task, and measures related to emergent literacy, vocabulary, and early math skills. The results of the quantitative study suggest that "children with higher behavioral regulation achieved significantly higher levels in emergent literacy, vocabulary, and math skills" (2007, p. 955). In addition, the level of growth shown in self-regulation skills predicted the level of growth in academic skills. Results also showed student growth in attention, working memory, and inhibitory control (McClelland et al., 2007).

Blair and Razza (2007) suggest that self-regulation, particularly peer self-regulation, showed positive associations with literacy outcomes. They conducted a study with preschool students in which self-regulation measures and literacy abilities were measured. The study, which included 170 students, tested participants during two sessions during the school year. The participating students were measured for self-regulation, literacy, and math. Results suggest that various aspects of self-regulation were correlated to aspects of letter recognition and letter knowledge. Blair and Razza (2007) also suggest that self-regulation and phonemic awareness could become more prominent as students in school develop and make progress toward literacy skills. Students with lower levels of self-regulation tend to exhibit more disruptive behavior and create more disruptions in classroom learning. The resulting reduction in instruction affects students' literacy skills. In addition, specific skills, such as decoding, text processing, and fluency in word recognition, contribute to overall comprehension and academic achievement; these results suggest a relation to students' levels of regulation. Self-regulation and student engagement appear to have a connection; less motivation is a result of lower levels of regulating one's own attention and maintaining engagement in learning

Similarly, Cameron and Morrison (2011) conducted a five-year longitudinal study in which preschool students were videotaped and tested on measures of self-regulation and academics. Parents of participating students were given questionnaires that inquired about demographic information. Researchers also tested participants on general knowledge, mathematics, emergent literacy skills, and vocabulary. The first testing session was during year two of the study, which was when students entered kindergarten. The second testing session was during year three of the study when participating students began first grade. The students were tested with measures of self-regulation, mathematics, reading readiness, and vocabulary outcome assessments. After the two years of testing, students were then videotaped in the classroom in order to measure the amount of teachers' orienting. "Orienting" here was defined as teachers' ability to explain and demonstrate activities and expectations to young students. Results suggest that students in classrooms where teachers oriented them well also performed better on self-regulation and literacy assessments. This study also suggests that there is a connection between self-regulation and overall academics as it relates to proper expectations and explanations portrayed by teachers.

Self-regulation allows children to follow and comply with rules, manage emotions, and carry out problem-solving tasks on their own. These skills are of particular importance to young children entering formal schooling. For Latinx preschoolers who are acquiring more than one language simultaneously, understanding the association between language, academic competence, and regulatory skills is central to their development.

Latinx Parenting, Self-Regulation, and Latinx Preschoolers

As this chapter has shown, self-regulation allows children to follow and comply with rules, manage emotions, and carry out problem-solving tasks on their own, and these skills are of particular importance to young children entering formal schooling. Understanding the association between language, academic competence, and regulatory skills is central to the development of Latinx preschoolers, who are acquiring more than one language simultaneously. As the number of Latinx young children increases, knowledge regarding the role of parenting in these children's development will prove useful in several contexts, such as daycare centers, early intervention programs, parenting workshops, and schools. Most studies assessing the effects of parental disciplining behaviors on young children have been carried out with non-Latinx families, and little research has looked at the way these behaviors affect Latinx children (Halgunseth et al. 2009). Consequently, understanding the core values of *educación*, *familismo*, and *respeto* and how to support them is critical to development in the classroom.

Educación, Familismo, and Respeto

To review these values, which were introduced in Chapter 1, *educación* (education) is a term that has a much broader meaning in Spanish than it does in English. In addition to academic education, the term also refers to good manners, high morals, honesty, politeness, respectfulness, and responsibility. Cultivating values of morality and responsibility in children is a central objective in the child-rearing goals of Latinx parents (Fracasso & Busch-Rossnagel, 1992). This is highly informative in the context of parental engagement, as many of the activities that Latinx parents do to support the education of young children include more than academics alone, incorporating social skills and positive interactions. It is also crucial for educators to understand that, in the Latinx community, the term *familismo* comprises the idea that the family is the primary site for the resolution of any problems or concerns that might arise. As a result, Latinx families may believe that people from outside the family should not have a role in decision-making related to a child's general well-being, mental health, or social-emotional development. This could include situations in which a child has a learning difference or another problem hampering their academic performance. Even in such a situation, on account of *familismo*, some Latinx families may seem to resist educators' efforts to make recommendations or assist in realms such as a child's social development, happiness, and well-being, as these are traditionally understood to belong in the realm of the family. *Respeto* (literally, "respect") refers to the maintenance of harmonious interpersonal relationships through respect for others. Included in this "respect" is respect for the role(s) of each family member. From a young age, many children from Latinx families are taught and expected to show respect for elders, meaning to address them politely and refrain from challenging their opinions and interrupting them (Fracasso & Busch-Rossnagel, 1992). The value of *respeto* also prizes showing deference for professionals and experts. Traditionally, Latinxs treat teachers and educators with great respect, and, therefore, Latinx parents are often reluctant to challenge a school's authority, as it goes against their ideas about authority and respect (Smith et al., 2008). Similarly, parents might not feel it is appropriate to ask questions and might defer to their children's teachers and other educators. They may not feel it is compatible with *respeto* to act as an equal partner with these educators, that is, to share the power of decision-making or make suggestions about the curriculum, programs, or services. Since the American model of parental engagement, by contrast, assumes that parents should act (or at least want and try to act) as partners, Latinx families may look disengaged to educators who are not aware of *respeto*. Likewise, Latinx parents often view this respect and authority as a two-way street. Parents respect educators' teaching decisions, and, in turn, they expect educators to respect their child-rearing decisions. Educators' questioning of parental involvement can thus be perceived as a disrespectful critique (Delgado-Gaitan, 2004).

Self-Regulation and Self-Assertion, Compliance, and Discipline

Self-Regulation

Self-regulation constitutes the child's ability to successfully manage emotional and cognitive states during stressful or demanding situations and to engage in successful interactions with peers and adults. As children develop, they need to find a balance between their ability to exhibit self-regulation and their desire for self-assertion. Latinx family practices can serve as key models for teaching regulatory behavior, as positive or negative family-rearing practices are influenced by one's culture. Families can shape the language needed to communicate and express emotions.

Research has suggested that Latinx families are likely to use a higher level of intervention and control when parenting, than non-Latinx families. Additionally, Diemer et al. (2021) found that in Latinx families, there was much more physical control during play, learning, and activities of daily living. But, with regards to the issue of acculturation, in Latinx families, when higher-level parental intrusion is present, the parental level of acculturation matters. In particular, some studies have indicated that mothers with lower levels of acculturation controlling behaviors, such as intrusiveness and physical and verbal discipline, may have fewer negative or positive implications for children's development compared to those same behaviors from more acculturated mothers (Ispa et al., 2004; Kim et al., 2018; Wood & Grau 2018). This may happen because, within Latinx communities, there is a sense of belonging that influences the way in which young learners understand others' actions and the ways in which they communicate with their peers. In particular, Latinx families foster the notion that children need to be well-behaved in all social contexts and to be respectful to the adults with whom they interact. Children are taught to respect and defer to decisions that come from others (including their mothers) based on age, sex, and position of authority.

Through this framework of Latinx upbringing, the way young children learn to control their emotions, behavior, and cognition is based on Latinx family foundations. Latinx people value the family to the extent that it is part of one individual identity that fosters a sense of belonging in the early years. Young learners are taught early that Latinx families are extended ones that include relatives such as grandparents, aunts, uncles, cousins, and even individuals who are not biologically related to, but support, the family. Decisions in the Latinx home often involve a collective opinion from all family members; this differs from decision-making processes in most Western family cultures.

Self-Assertion

Self-assertion is the child's intrinsic motivation toward a goal-directed behavior, which involves a child's intention, will, and autonomy. This dimension of the self develops during the toddler years when the child gains a sense of independence as a result of their increased physical autonomy (DesRosiers, 1998). As children grow, they increasingly find pleasure in activities they can accomplish on their own. When children insist on accomplishing a task in an independent manner and resist help, they are asserting their will. Similarly, when a child refuses to comply with the goals and expectations of others, this is also a child's assertion of will (DesRosiers, 1998).

Compliance and Non-Compliance

Compliance is considered to be a reflection of self-regulation, as it involves the child's ability to regulate behaviors in response to external demands (Kochanska et al., 2001). Compliance is most frequently observed in mother-child interactions; however, it can be extended to varied social interactions (Feldman & Klein, 2003). In addition to compliance, children exhibit several forms of non-compliance, including refusal, defiance, and passive non-compliance.

Refusal to comply is generally seen as a behavioral expression of self-assertion (Crockenberg & Litman, 1990; Pettygrove et al., 2013). The research proposes that toddlers reacting with resistance to adults' controlling behaviors should not be considered obstinate but, rather, motivated to be autonomous and control their environment (Dix et al., 2007). As children enter the second year of life, they develop a sense of autonomy and assertiveness, which motivates children to control and affect outcomes, especially when those outcomes seem to affect their well-being. Children begin to refuse by saying no to parental commands and exhibit other forms of resistance by asserting their own will.

Defiance is non-compliance combined with negative effects, such as anger or resentment. This type of non-compliance is a reflection of the child's motivation to resist parental goals, not of the assertion of his or her will (Crockenberg & Litman, 1990; Pettygrove et al., 2013). Crockenberg and Litman (1990) propose that refusals are conceptually different from defiance, in that refusals are seen as a sign of higher competence and more autonomy than defiance because the child's motivation is self-assertion, rather than resisting the parents' goals (Dix et al., 2007).

Passive non-compliance involves the child's disregard of parental controls without a direct confrontation or acknowledgment of the conflict and the incompatible goals (Dix et al., 2007). This form of non-compliance is an indicator of low assertiveness and thus is not a reflection of self-assertion. This form of non-compliance has been found to be common among children of severely impaired mothers, including depressed mothers (Crockenberg & Litman, 1990).

Compliance, refusal, and defiance in children are related to distinctive parenting behaviors in parenting cultures, whether in Latinx or North American culture. However, when it comes to children's refusal, knowledge gathered from children in other cultural contexts does not generalize to Latinx students. The development of children's self-regulation and self-assertion is supported by the role of parenting in the development of these skills. As a result, the importance of parenting behaviors in the development of children's compliance and defiance can be informative in the design and implementation of behavioral interventions targeting Latinx children and their families, including parenting workshops, home visitations, and family engagement activities. Assertiveness is highly valued in Western culture, including in its school systems, where the ability to refuse help is considered an indication of maturity and independence. Latinx children might find it difficult to refuse or to challenge an adult's perspective even when this is a desirable practice in the larger culture of which they are a part. Thus, expressions of refusal might not be viewed as positive in Latinx families and might not be reproduced by Latinx children in educational settings.

Disciplining Behaviors

Latinx families differ from Western families in the behaviors they use when socializing their children to cope with adults' expectations. Parental control has long-lasting effects on children's development of self-regulation, self-assertion, compliance, and non-compliance. Research has shown that negative disciplining behaviors have a negative impact on self-regulation and self-assertion in children. Parental negative disciplining behaviors have been associated with low achievement and lower levels of autonomy in young children (DesRosiers, 1998). Mothers' use of power control strategies, such as physical enforcement and infrequent use of positive reinforcement, predicts passive non-compliance in children. Additionally, parental control practices that are extremely power-assertive, such as harshness, criticism, and excessive physical intervention, are associated with defiant behaviors (Crockenberg & Litman, 1990; Pettygrove et al., 2013). Similarly, physical punishment has the most dramatic effect on children; mothers who relied on physical punishment had toddlers who were more likely to ignore prohibitions and actively disobey maternal controls. The results found that physical punishment is an ineffective way to teach compliance and impulse control; it interferes with the child's development of self-regulation.

On the other hand, positive control and disciplining behaviors are associated with positive outcomes in young children. For example, supportive verbal communication by mothers has been associated with higher levels of autonomy in young children (DesRosiers, 1998). Additionally, positive verbal control has been associated with high levels of self-regulation and compliance in young children (Kuczynski & Kochanska, 1990). Similarly, maternal justification, negotiations, and the use of explanations involving emotions predicted internalization and self-regulation in children.

Although compliance is related to positive parenting, children who experience positive parenting tend to be more autonomous and assertive and are more likely to assert their will successfully and refuse to comply with parental control. Dix and colleagues (2007) found that mothers' supportive and autonomy-granting behaviors resulted in children who refused to comply with maternal demands. In turn, they propose that active resistance to parental control can be a reflection of self-assertion and an indication of positive parenting.

In sum, parents have a great impact on the way children develop self-assertion, self-regulation, compliance, and non-compliance. Parental positive disciplining behaviors predict compliance, and negative disciplining behaviors predict defiance. However, non-compliance, especially in the form of refusal, can be an indicator of self-assertion, autonomy, and positive parenting (Kochanska et al., 2001). Latinx practices influence young children's developmental processes of negotiating their independence and self-assertion while responding to adults' set goals.

Summary

Self-regulation skills have positive effects on Latinx preschool children both academically and emotionally. As previously stated, the ability to self-regulate is a better indicator of school readiness in younger learners. However, this is particularly important to Latinx DLLs as the development of language and self-regulatory skills are key factors during the preschool years; yet there is a paucity of research that looks at the associations in Latinx children much less quantitative data to support the needs of this population.

· 4 ·

CURRENT DATA ON SELF-REGULATION IN LATINX PRESCHOOLERS

The previous chapter discussed the critical association of self-regulation. This chapter will discuss the current research that was conducted to provide data that can support Latinx DLL children. Vygotsky suggests that preschool children can learn to regulate through the internalizing of private speech into their inner regulating thoughts, suggesting the importance of language and self-regulation. Nevertheless, is this association also one that can be found in Latinx preschoolers who are DLL?

The results from the data collected for this research from Latinx preschoolers show significant associations between self-regulation and language in Latinx preschoolers. Especially interesting was the association found between Latinx preschoolers' language skills over time in relation to cognitive skills and their impulses over time in the classroom. Prior to discussing the data of this investigation and how it impacts pedagogy, the quantitative data needs to be examined. As previously stated, there is a paucity of research looking at self-regulation in Latinx students but even more limited is the quantitative data available to help answer the aforementioned questions.

Method

To better understand the association between Latinx preschoolers, self-regulation, and language skills, a pre- and post-investigation were conducted with a total of 32 Latinx preschoolers residing in a lower-Socioeconomic Status (SES) and ethnically diverse community. Both preschool curricula strongly support extended blocks of either indoor or outdoor play for the students. Explicitly, the focus was on observing if Latinx preschoolers' self-regulation would increase as their language skills also increased during a time interval of six months. The investigation took on a quasi-experimental design, in which participants were given pretests (Time 1) and posttests (Time 2) during the school year.

Participants

The parents or guardians of this current research needed to identify the students as Latinx DLL preschoolers through a home language survey given by the board of education during enrollment. In addition to families identifying their children as Latinx DLLs, teachers had to provide an evaluation of students' language levels. The second survey the teachers completed required them to identify the level of English language proficiency of the participating Latinx students. This survey was created using five stages involved in second language acquisition. Through this framework this five-stage developmental survey explicitly describes each of the five language stages as: (a) Stage 1—home language use, (b) Stage 2—nonverbal; child communicates with gestures and actions, (c) Stage 3—telegraphic and formulaic speech; child communicates using one or two words or short phrases, (d) Stage 4—productive language; child understands most of what is being said in the classroom, and speaks in longer phrases and complete sentences, with frequent word errors, and (e) Stage 5—fluent English user; child speaks English in most social and learning contexts. Language at this stage is still challenging in content areas. This survey showed what language stage students demonstrated at the time of enrollment.

Based on the parental survey and teacher language evaluations, of the 32 student participants, approximately 60% fell within levels 1 and 3. These results suggest that Latinx preschoolers are entering preschool with lower levels of English language skills than their English-only-speaking peers and are placed in classrooms with educators who may or may not be able to support

Table 1: Demographic Characteristics of the Sample

Variable	DLL (n = 32)	%
Gender		
Male	19	59
Female	13	41
Ethnicity		
Hispanic/Latino	28	88
African-American	4	13
Language	9	29
English		
Spanish	23	72
Language Level	7	22
Stage 1		
Stage 2	5	16
Stage 3	7	22
Stage 4	5	16
Stage 5	8	25

a biliterate, bilingual, and bicultural environment. This further supports the idea that Latinx students who are falling behind continue to fall behind due to lacking support services and pedagogical practices in the classroom.

Setting

Data was collected from two preschool settings. Both settings were similar in SES and both curricula allowed for development through social and academic aspects. The first setting was a state-funded universal prekindergarten program (UPK) in a low-income, ethnically diverse district. The program offered three classes of morning and afternoon half-day sessions. The morning session hours were from 8:50 a.m. to 11:30 a.m. while the afternoon session hours were from 12:45 p.m. to 3:00 p.m. The teachers in the district implemented the *Tools of the Mind* (TOM) curriculum. The TOM program holds self-regulatory activities as the foundation of any learning activity that takes place in the classroom. This program allowed for social interaction as a leading learning experience. The classrooms in this study specifically allowed the students 30 minutes of play activities. The TOM curriculum provides monthly themes to teach oral language and literacy skills.

The second school was a federally funded Head Start program. The Head Start is located in the same ethnically diverse community as the UPK public school program. This Head Start setting had a total of five classes. Both schools were similar in SES, ethnicity and language proficiencies. Similar to the UPK, the Head Start also offered the students one class that had a morning and afternoon program while the remaining four classrooms were full-day programs from 9:00 a.m. to 3:00 p.m. This setting implemented a preschool program called *Creative Curriculum*. *Creative Curriculum* is primarily focused on providing a social-emotional-based experience in learning. This program allowed for social interaction opportunities among preschool children as a means of developing and acquiring new skills. Students in this setting were allowed to play for 30 minutes in the classroom. The play centers in this program were not explicitly related to any particular theme.

Instrumentation

To look into the associations between language and self-regulation in Latinx preschoolers, several English and Spanish standardized assessments were implemented, and these assessments were given to the student participants twice during the school year. Table 2 summarizes the assessments used in this research.

PRSA

Self-regulation measures allowed for a clearer understanding of the normative development of participants, and they provided a structured measurement. The Preschool Self-Regulation Assessment (PSRA) is a battery of self-regulatory tasks adapted from Murray and Kochanska's (2002) effortful control and executive control tasks. Further, it is a one-on-one direct assessment measure that was developed to evaluate self-regulatory skills in preschool students. The tasks were developed to assess children's (a) attention and planning skills, (b) impulse control, (c) ability to follow directions, and (d) emotional responses. These tasks were adapted from well-validated, lab-based measures of preschoolers' self-regulation (Smith-Donald et al., 2007). The tasks offer a standardized direct assessment of young children's self-regulation (Smith-Donald et al., 2007). Specifically, the following tasks were used to measure students' self-regulation abilities (see Table 3).

Table 2: Table Summary from Scores Obtained

Assessments		Description
GRTR		*Get Ready To Read* measures print/phonological skills.
EOWPVT-4 EOWPVT-Spanish		EOWPVT-4 is an expressive vocabulary test in English. EOWPVT-Spanish is an expressive test in Spanish. Based on each student's ceiling score and their chronological age they are assigned to the percentile rank they fall into
ROWPVT-4 ROWPVT-Spanish		ROWPVT-4 is a receptive vocabulary test in English. ROWPVT-Spanish is a receptive test in Spanish. Based on each student's ceiling score and their chronological age they are assigned to the percentile rank they fall into.
Pre-IPT Oral		Pre-Idea Proficiency Test. Evaluates oral speaking proficiency
PSRA	Pencil tap	Cognitive Regulation
	Tower Task	Cognitive Regulation
	Toy Wrap	Impulse Regulation
	Toy Wrap Wait	Impulse Regulation
	Snack Delay	Impulse Regulation
	Tongue Task	Impulse Regulation

Pencil Tap Task

This task was not timed. It asked the students to go through a teaching trial before the actual trial. Rules for the task were reviewed, followed by a brief practice session. The rules for this activity were that when the examiner tapped the pencil once on the table, the students tapped twice, and when the examiner tapped twice, the student needed to tap only once. After students understood the rules, a scored trial was conducted. In the actual trial, there were 16 taps that the student completed. During the actual trial, students were not reminded of the rules or given any type of praise by the examiner.

Tower Task

This task had a practice and actual trial. During the practice trial, the student was told they would build a tower together with the examiner, each taking a turn until the tower was completed. For the practice portion, only six blocks were used. The examiner and student each took a turn adding one block to the tower. The examiner reminded the student of the rule during the practice trials when the student forgot to give the examiner a turn. Once the practice trial using six blocks was completed, the examiner proceeded to the actual trial. The actual trial consisted of 12 blocks and the same turn-taking rule. However, the examiner was not allowed to remind the student of the rule during the actual trial.

Toy Wrap, Toy Wait Task

For this task, the student was asked to turn their chair so that they were not facing the examiner. The examiner then pretended to wrap up a toy and made noises with the wrapping paper to try and get the student's attention. If the child peeked, the examiner noted the time of peeking. After a minute, the examiner asked the student to turn around. The examiner put materials away while the wrapped toy was on the table with the student facing the toy. The students had to wait one minute until they could touch the toy. The examiner noted if the student touched the toy before the one-minute wait. Once that minute was up, the examiner allowed the child to play with the toy.

Snack Delay Task

The student had to keep both hands flat on the table until the examiner instructed the student to take a goldfish cracker from the *delay* cup and place it into another cup for them to eat later. The task had four scored and timed trials. The first trial was a 10-second hold, and the student could move the goldfish cracker into their cup. The second trial was 20 seconds, the third was 30 seconds, and the last was 60 seconds.

Tongue Task

The tongue task required the student to hold the goldfish cracker on their tongue for 10 seconds during the practice trial. The actual trial consisted of the student holding the goldfish cracker on their tongue. The examiner and the student held the snack on their tongues without chewing it, swallowing it, or dropping it. The examiner was allowed to correct and praise the children during the practice trials. During these practices, the children could

Table 3: Summary of PSRA Tasks

Task	Description	Targeted self-regulation skills
Pencil Tap	Tap 1 time when I tap 2 times	Cognitive Control
Turn Task	Take turns adding blocks	Cognitive Control
Toy Wrap	Don't peek while wrapping surprise	Impulse control
Toy Wrap Wait	Wait to open surprise	Impulse control
Snack Delay	Wait for a beep to get snack	Impulse control
Tongue Task	Hold snack on tongue w/o eating	Impulse control

follow directions and complete each task. However, when the examiner was not allowed to repeat the rules/instructions in the scored trials, the children had difficulties completing some of the tasks individually.

GRTR

Get Ready to Read (GRTR) is a criterion-referenced assessment that screens preschool children's development in emergent literacy skills. This test is also available in Spanish for non-English speaking students. It specifically measures print knowledge and phonological awareness.

Expressive and Receptive Vocabulary Assessments: The EOWPVT-4

Vocabulary assessments were administered individually to all participants. A Spanish version was administered to Spanish-speaking participants. The Expressive One-Word Picture Vocabulary English and Expressive One-Word Picture Vocabulary Spanish are norm-referenced assessments that measure the English- and Spanish-speaking vocabulary of preschool children. The tests consist of illustrations, with each one representing an object, action, or concept. The raw scores obtained were used to report standard scores and percentile ranks.

Language Measures: Three Assessments

Administering a single test to measure language in Latinx preschoolers does not allow for accurate performance regarding language abilities (Castro et al., 2013; Leung & Brice, 2013). It is important to look at vocabulary, oral language, written language, phonology, morphology, syntax, and semantics (Leung & Brice, 2013). In this study, to better account for language, a number of assessments were used to evaluate Latinx preschoolers' abilities in expressive and receptive language skills: the above-mentioned EOWPVT-4/EOWPVT-Spanish; the Pre-Idea Proficiency Test (Pre-IPT) of oral and vocabulary skills; and the Receptive One-Word Picture Vocabulary English (ROWPVT-4)/Receptive One-Word Picture Vocabulary Spanish (ROWPVT-Spanish). The Pre-IPT–Oral Tests assessed proficiency in four domains of oral language: vocabulary, grammar, comprehension, and verbal expression.

Procedures

Prior to the commencement of the study, The Institutional Review Board (IRB), approved all materials and assessments as proposed. Questionnaires used in this study can be found in Appendix A. Permission was granted by the authors of the PSRA measures to administer these tasks without the required one-day training workshop (Dr. Cybele Raver). The training materials were gathered and reviewed before implementing the assessments. Parents were provided with letters and permission slips explaining the focus of the study. The letters described and asked parents if their child could be assessed in order to collect data pertaining to self-regulation skills. The letters also ensured parents that participants' information and identity would be kept anonymous and confidential and that withdrawal at any time from the study would not be a problem. Once the sample of participants was collected, language surveys from parents and language acquisition surveys from teachers were examined to determine DLL students and their English language levels. When DLL classification was determined, students were tested either in English or Spanish with self-regulation, literacy, and language measures for Time 1. After six months, students were re-administered the assessments for Time 2 evaluations.

The PSRA tasks were standardized and a composite score for two different types of self-regulation were conducted. Scores for PSRA Turn Task (TRT) and Pencil Task (PT) were computed under the cognitive control variable. Scores for PSRA Toy Wait (TW), Toy Wrap Wait (TWW), Snack Delay (SD), and Tongue Task (TT) were computed under the impulse control variable.

Computation of a composite impulse and cognitive control variable was vital to this study as each variable not only is distinguishable, both neutrally and behaviorally but distinct theoretically and practically as well. In addition, the variables for impulse and cognitive control were correlated for Time 1 and Time 2 to ensure that these two aspects of self-regulation measured different skills. Correlations suggest that these two variables do measure different types of self-regulation, as the correlation coefficients were less than 0.8. Therefore, variables classified under impulse control and variables under cognitive control were kept as two separate variables and measurements of self-regulation.

Similarly, for the language measures, a composite vocabulary score was also calculated. The expressive and receptive standard scores were combined to form Time 1 and Time 2

composite values. This value explicitly measures vocabulary skills of preschool students and was used throughout this study for further statistical analyses. In addition to previous research, preliminary correlations were also conducted to determine and to ensure that the variables that made up the vocabulary variable and the oral language proficiency variable measured different aspects of language. For both Time 1 and Time 2, the results from the correlation coefficients between vocabulary and the oral proficiency variables were reviewed. Overall the correlations produced coefficients less than 0.8, suggesting that these variables measure two different aspects of language. Therefore, the decision to keep these two variables separate was also supported.

Results: Associations Between Latinx Preschoolers' Language Skills and Self-Regulation

The relationship between self-regulation skills, cognitive and impulse control, and language acquisition skills in Latinx preschoolers was measured by vocabulary and oral proficiency. Table 4 summarizes the mean and standard deviations for the variables used in this research. These two tables highlight the change in development that occurred among Latinx students. It shows that as students developed more oral skills and vocabulary, the deviations from the higher means were reduced, suggesting less variability in language skills.

Further analyses were conducted to measure the associations that Latinx preschooler language had with self-regulation. Two one-tailed Pearson r correlations were used to measure the strength of the linear association between the emergent language skills and self-regulation variables. One was conducted at the beginning of the school year, and the second one was conducted six months after the students had started school.

Results from Time 1

The results from the beginning of the school year imply that cognitive control and oral language proficiency have a significant positive correlation ($r = 0.528$, $p < 0.01$). However, at this time in Latinx preschoolers' development, these two variables have a moderate association of 28%, suggesting that scores in language proficiency can only explain 28% of students' performance in cognitive control. Cognitive control allows young learners to focus on the content presented at school and thus contend with fewer distractions. This, in other words, is the ability to consciously pay attention and learn. During this first interval, cognitive control was shown to be statistically correlated with vocabulary ($r = 0.316$, $p < 0.01$) but with very low strength or association (9%) in the relationship between the variables.

At the time that students were first tested and then again during the year, they attended their programs and continued to learn the content provided to them. They were not offered any language services or bilingual curricula, but the teachers fully supported the concept of play and allowed social interactions among all students in the class.

Results from Time 2

The second correlation took place after students had been in the classroom for six months. The results showed that cognitive control and oral language proficiency had a significant positive correlation ($r = 0.687$, $p < 0.01$). Unlike Time 1, the strength of the relationship between the scores was strong, with a 47% proportion of variance between students' cognitive scores and variance in scores of oral language proficiency. In this case, oral language proficiency scores can have a much higher association than at the beginning of the school year. Cognitive control was again correlated with vocabulary, and it was also statistically correlated with vocabulary ($r = 0.589$, $p < 0.01$). Again, the strength of the relationship between the scores is strong, and approximately 35% of the proportion of variance is associated between cognitive scores and vocabulary scores. Cognitive control and vocabulary increased from 9% to 25% in six months for Latinx preschoolers. One additional result that also was significant for Latinx preschoolers was the association between impulse control and oral language proficiency. Different from cognitive control, impulse control is the ability of students to control their emotions and behaviors. Impulse control and oral language proficiency revealed a significant positive correlation ($r = 0.610$, $p < 0.01$). The strength of the relationship between the

Table 4: Mean and Standard Deviations for Self-Regulation and Language Skills Time 1 and Time 2

Measure	M1	SD1	M2	SD2
Cognitive Control	-0.27	0.73	-0.14	1.06
Impulse Control	-0.10	0.58	-0.08	0.88
Language Skills	61.41	20.47	91.56	23.34
Vocabulary Skills	80.31	15.20	90.41	11.45

Note. n = 32

Table 5: Correlations for Self-Regulation and Language Skills Time 1 and 2

	Time 1				Time 2			
Measure	1	2	3	4	1	2	3	4
Cognitive Control								
Impulse Control	0.307**				0.886**			
Oral Language	0.528**	0.348**			0.687**	0.610**		
Vocabulary Skills	0.316*	0.095	453**		0.589**	0.415**	0.646**	

Note. n = 32. ** $p < 0.01$ level (1-tailed). * $p < 0.05$ level (1-tailed).

scores was moderately strong during Time 2. Therefore, there is a 37% proportion of variance associated between impulse scores and variance in scores of oral language proficiency. Impulse control was also statistically correlated with vocabulary ($r = 0.415$, $p < 0.01$). Thus, approximately 17% of the proportion of variance is associated between impulse scores and vocabulary scores. The association at Time 2 suggests that as language skills are developed, the scores in language measures can be used to predict scores in self-regulation measures. The strength of the relationships between language and self-regulation in Latinx preschoolers was higher than in Time 1.

Analysis of Time 1 and Time 2 Results: Self-Regulation and Academic Achievement

The findings reveal that all participants made gains in scores for all literacy assessments over time. The results suggest that self-regulation and literacy yielded positive and significant associations with impulse, cognitive control, and emergent literacy skills. This finding further supports the existence of a relationship between impulse and cognitive control and emergent literacy skills. Specifically, the results of this investigation reveal that there are significant associations between cognitive control and literacy, print/phonological awareness ($r = 0.495$, $p < 0.001$), and vocabulary ($r = 0.504$, $p < 0.001$). Based on the correlations, 50% of the variance in emergent literacy skills can be attributed to cognitive control in Time 2.

Cognitive control is the ability to consciously control attention and memory processes (Bronson, 2000); consciously recalling, from memory, literacy skills such as the alphabet and names and sounds of letters is part of cognitive control. Paying attention to sounds and being aware of sound segments in spoken language is another part of cognitive control (Muller et al., 2009). The fact that this investigation related higher levels of cognitive regulatory skills with higher levels of literacy skills, as revealed in Time 2, can be interpreted to show that emergent literacy skills in preschool relate to the practice of attention control and memory.

Analysis of Time 1 and Time 2 Results: Self-Regulation and Language Acquisition Skills

The growth of the bilingual population poses a myriad of obstacles as to how to address the linguistic and socialization needs of Latinx preschoolers. Early childhood programs have the capacity to promote development in Latinx preschoolers through sociocultural contexts and the need to strive to address the social needs of Latinx preschoolers (Castro et al., 2013; Luchtel et al., 2010).

Latinx participants in this investigation made gains in scores for self-regulation and language measures over time. Growth between Time 1 and Time 2 in self-regulation related to the gains in language children made between Time 1 and Time 2. Specifically, between language and cognitive control, associations were stronger for Time 2 (oral proficiency [$r = 0.687$, $p < 0.01$] and vocabulary [$r = 0.589$, $p < 0.01$]). This result is supported by findings in McClelland et al.'s study (2007) that suggest that students showing growth in self-regulation from Time 1 and Time 2 demonstrated gains in vocabulary between Time 1 and Time 2. Stronger correlation strengths between cognitive control and language suggest that cognitive control has more prevalent associations than impulse control in the development of language in Latinx preschoolers. Approximately 82% of the variance in language can be attributed to cognitive control in Time 2. The interpretation of this finding can be derived from the concept that "language leads to consciousness, but then it is the conscious use of language in self-directed speech that allows children to exercise control over thoughts, actions, and emotions" (Muller et al., 2009, p. 57). Cognitive control involves abilities in cognitive flexibility, working memory, and planning (Muller et al., 2009). Planning is related to verbal abilities, as children organize and plan their behaviors by first internalizing aspects of language to self-regulate (Muller et al., 2009). Although Willoughby et al. (2011) did not sample Latinx preschoolers, their correlation results also suggest that cognitive control had stronger associations with phonological awareness in preschool students. The positive correlation results of this study can further be interpreted through the associations described by Vygotsky of "inner speech," leading to the internalization of verbal thoughts to self-regulate. In other words, inner speech turns into inner thoughts that later regulate and play a major role in academics and social abilities.

Overall, all participants' scores improved from Time 1 to Time 2. The results of the analysis indicate that there is a significant positive association between self-regulation and language skills. Suggesting that the ability of Latinx preschoolers to self-regulate can be positively associated with the acquisition of language skills. Concurrently, these findings also indicate that cognitive control has higher correlations with language than impulse control. Therefore, as language develops in Latinx preschoolers, so do cognitive regulation skills.

What Do the Findings Mean?

The results suggest that in Latinx children, as their language skills developed, so did their ability to self-regulate. Specifically, their ability to focus on classroom tasks with fewer distractions had a stronger link to expressive and receptive language skills. As children developed more expressive skills, they were able to use private speech to control impulses and behaviors. Private speech or self-talk is eventually internalized into thought, and as children age, the need to use language to solve problems is not needed as much. However, since regulatory thoughts have not been internalized in young children, language is used as a form of self-regulation. As Latinx students were allowed to socialize and gain more vocabulary to use as their regulating tool, their cognitive control increased. Additionally, as Latinx students developed receptive skills in both languages, they could better understand rules and cause-and-effect relationships, such as consequences for their behaviors and actions. These results also suggest that language and self-regulation are related through specific functions. Both language and self-regulation share components of cognitive flexibility and working memory.

Cognitive flexibility is the ability to adapt to changes and change tasks that are unplanned. Cognitive flexibility is also referred to as task switching, which is an ability that DLLs learn early on. Latinx DLLs who are developing two languages, unlike adding a second language, have both languages active in the brain. Latinx DLLs learn to control which language they will respond with, given their environmental context. This is not a skill that monolingual children learn to regulate as they do not have two or more languages from which to choose when engaging in either expressive or receptive language.

The second shared component between self-regulation and language is working memory. Working memory, or specifically verbal working memory, is the processing of information. This allows students to convert speech to meaning and store that information. Working memory is based on the attentional control given by an individual. Hence, as the results suggest, increasing language skills promotes higher verbal working memory, allowing for further attentional control or cognitive regulation practices.

In order for DLLs to develop this skill, both languages need to be supported. The Long Island Index (2013) reported that approximately one in every four students in low SES school districts possessed limited English language abilities. Children who come from low SES communities are at risk for entering kindergarten with low levels of self-regulation. Although income was not examined in this study, it should be noted that Latinx DLLs in this study came from school settings geographically located in low SES communities. Therefore, the results of this investigation can provide direction and proper implementation of strategies for DLLs in low SES settings. The growth of the bilingual population poses a myriad of obstacles on how to address the linguistic and socialization needs of Latinx children. Early childhood programs have the capacity to promote development in DLLs through sociocultural contexts and need to strive to address the social needs of DLLs; a current issue we face is how these aforementioned programs can support these DLL Latinx participants in this investigation made gains in scores for self-regulation and language measures over time, specifically between language and cognitive control; this suggests that "language leads to consciousness, but then it is the conscious use of language in self-directed speech that allows children to exercise control over thoughts, actions, and emotions" (Muller et al., 2009, p. 57). Cognitive control involves abilities in cognitive flexibility, working memory, and planning. Planning is related to verbal abilities as children organize and plan their behaviors by first internalizing aspects of language to self-regulate. The positive correlation results of this study can be further interpreted, through the associations described by Vygotsky, as "inner speech," which is the internalization of verbal thoughts to facilitate self-regulation. Language acts as a mediating tool to control and regulate cognition, behavior, and emotions. Vygotsky stated that inner speech turns into inner thoughts that later regulate and play a major role in academics and in social abilities.

Results, Regimes of Truth, and Vygotsky

The concept that power is held at the state and federal level, and that learning standards regulate preschool curricula, were both noted. Foucault describes the process of normalization as those acts and practices that seem normal. In education, this notion presented by Foucault relates to educators who follow curricula "regulated" through the "power" of educational policies, without questioning the lack of focus on skills that could potentially benefit development. Normalization is the process of conforming to current learning standards and then measuring child development to these set norms in education.

The current preschool curriculum focuses on academics as an indicator of achievement, as policies revolve around accountability and measures of standardized assessments.

Vygotsky's framework also related the importance of self-regulation to academic skills, such as language and literacy as a key focus. Despite growing research and perspectives from the Vygotskian framework, the lack of emphasis on regulatory skill has been accepted as an appropriate educational practice today. Educational policies are inextricably linked to aspects of normalization in education. Until new "regimes of truth" are established through research, current policies will continue to disregard the need for the development of regulation skills in preschool and particularly as they relate to DLLs.

The results of statistically significant correlations in this investigation between language and self-regulation support recent interest in self-regulatory skills in preschool children and in "new knowledge" as stated by the Foucaultian framework. Based on Foucault, these positive correctional results can be utilized to provide evidence for educators to question current curricula, encouraging a new direction and perhaps influence educational policies to focus on meeting the learning needs of Latinx children These results can contribute to a new set of "regimes of truth" that can replace the traditional didactic curricula and policies currently in place. Latinx children need the opportunity to develop through a social context where executive functions such as self-regulation skills are developed.

· 5 ·

IMPLEMENTING SELF-REGULATION PRACTICES FOR LATINX PRESCHOOLERS

Chapter 4 reported the results from the analyses conducted using Latinx students' Time 1 and Time 2 scores in self-regulation, literacy, and language. This chapter will summarize the purpose of the research and further elaborate on the findings and describe implications for practice. Positive and negative early childhood experiences influence the way in which each developmental domain progresses in young children (Ferjan Ramirez & Kuhl, 2017). Adverse childhood experiences (ACEs) have a great impact on young learners' development. In Latinx students, these adverse experiences can impede their language, social, and emotional development, hence affecting self-regulatory skills; these factors subsequently lead to lower levels of academic achievement. Therefore, ensuring that Latinx students' needs are being met in the preschool classroom is critical for their success.

This investigation took a close look at the relationship between self-regulation and Latinx preschoolers. Results support the links between self-regulation and language with Latinx participants. Hence, this study contributes to the body of current research relating to self-regulation and academics (Arslan et al., 2011; Blair, 2002; Day & Smith, 2013; Denham et al., 2012b; McClelland et al., 2007; Miller & Almon, 2009; Raver et al., 2011;

Rimm-Kaufman et al., 2009; Tominey & McClelland, 2011; Willoughby et al., 2011).

The results indicate that there needs to be a focus on how to support Latinx preschoolers in developing key skills that will determine their performance in later grades. Concurrently, results suggest that cognitive control has higher correlations with literacy than impulse control. Additional correlations between self-regulation and language suggest that the ability of Latinx preschoolers to regulate can be associated with the acquisition of language skills. Thus, these findings also imply that cognitive control has higher correlations with language than impulse control. This supports the Vygotskian framework of inner speech and how it then develops into inner thoughts in young children. These results also suggest practices that can better serve early childhood Latinx families, educators, and programs.

Current Educational Policies

Current educational policies, such as Common Core Standards (CCSS), do not allow educators to focus on cognitive control skills in preschools, even though they serve as indicators of school success. These CCSS primarily focus on constructional and academic types of activities in classrooms. As a result, under this policy, the developmental needs of the Latinx population are not met.

The results of statistically significant correlations in this investigation between language and self-regulation support recent interest in self-regulatory skills in preschool children and, in the words of the Foucaultian framework, "new knowledge" (Foucault, 1980). Using Foucault's perspective, these positive correctional results can be utilized to provide evidence for educators to question current curricula, encouraging a new direction and perhaps influencing educational policies to focus on meeting the sociocultural needs of the Latinx student (Lutchel et al., 2010). These results can contribute to a new set of "regimes of truth" that can replace the traditional didactic curricula and policies currently in place. Castro et al. (2013) and Lutchel et al. (2010) state that not having policies and curricula that reflect the needs of Latinx preschoolers means that these young students' needs are being disregarded. Latinx preschoolers need the opportunity to develop in a social context that encourages the development of executive functions, such as self-regulation skills.

Implications for Practice

Latinx preschoolers need a focused and tailored program to help them develop emotionally, behaviorally, and socially. Providing a positive environment during the preschool years is a way to offer Latinx preschoolers the opportunity to show gains in cognitive development. Specifically, providing a linguistically oriented program for Latinx preschoolers can promote academic readiness. However, there is no known program or curriculum that targets the development of higher-order thinking skills, specifically self-regulation, for Latinx preschoolers in preschools. Given the lower levels of participation of Latinx children in preschools, there needs to be a better way of addressing the cognitive gaps (Ferjan Ramirez & Kuhl, 2017). In particular, there needs to be involvement at the state and federal levels to better promote access to, and availability and awareness of, preschool and early childhood education programs for Latinx families.

Language in the Latinx Preschool Classroom

Focusing on language development, child-teacher interactions, and classroom quality supports the positive social development of the Latinx preschool student (Luchtel et al., 2010). Language proficiency is an indicator of social and emotional competencies. Lack of communication and expression, as well as lack of understanding of verbal direction, instruction, or classroom talk, can lead to negative socio-emotional development in young children. The results of the current study suggest that focusing in the early years on the development of language, whether it is in English or Spanish, can allow for better regulatory skills to develop.

Since, as mentioned above, Latinx people are currently the fastest-growing minority group in the United States, there is a need to adequately prepare teachers to support the academic and linguistic needs of Latinx students. In fact, it is critical to ensure that at least one Spanish-speaking educator is present at preschools teaching Latinx children. When Spanish is embedded into curricula, preschool programs can serve as an approach to help Latinx preschoolers and possibly improve self-regulation at this critical and sensitive age of development. It is imperative that schools provide a strong language program that can understand and is sensible to the needs of Latinx preschoolers and their family's language needs. The task of acquiring a second language is a difficult one, and therefore, having linguistic support can help ease the acquisition of both languages.

The positive correlation results in the study described in the last chapter showed that language is a factor in the development of cognitive self-regulation, which later impacts academic achievement in upper elementary grades. A number of other studies have also shown that the ability of Latinx preschoolers to socialize can positively impact their abilities to self-regulate and their academic achievement. In addition, as language skills in preschool children increase, their ability to socialize also increases. In addition, children who are allowed to develop proficiency in their native language while learning a second language are successful at social adaptation and autonomy.

Social Interactions in the Latinx Preschool Classroom

It is also important to focus on Latinx students' interactions with teachers in order to ensure children understand the cultural context and social interactions that are happening. Therefore, it is desirable to reduce classroom sizes, as that promotes greater teacher-student interaction and individualized education (Ferjan Ramirez & Kuhl, 2017). In addition, teachers need to maintain and encourage a positive social environment among Latinx preschoolers and support their relationships with all their peers and teachers in the classroom. Developing self-regulatory skills in a social context can become a challenge for Latinx preschoolers, who often do not have access to early social preschool programs that could help them learn to interact among a group with rules and expected behaviors. It seems that having teachers speak to them in their home language could help; those who had this not only received more individualized attention but formed a bond with the teacher; this bond positively influenced their behavior in the classroom, as well as their ability to interact better with their peers. This is consistent with the proposal of Vygotsky that executive functions, such as self-regulation, are developed through interpersonal interactions.

Play in the Latinx Preschool Classroom

The implementation of play can allow for the development of several skills at once, specifically: language, social interactions, impulse, and behavioral control. Ferjan Ramirez and Kuhl (2017) suggest that Latinx students need schools to design strategies to support active transport and increase student physical activity, such as outdoor learning, throughout the school day. Incorporating outdoor and indoor play can support Latinx students' developmental domains, as will be discussed in more detail below. Yet, preschools are limited in the amount of support and time they tend to give to play-based curricula. The pressures of CCSS and the related tests in elementary school have led preschool teachers to embed more programmatic and instructional practices. Although the New York State Prekindergarten Learning Standards (2011) acknowledge the importance of the social and emotional development of the preschool child in Domain 3, these skills are not the focus of the preschool curriculum. Domain 3 states that children are expected to regulate their responses to needs, feelings, and events. However, preschool teachers face the pressures of high stakes and accountability and are not given the opportunity to provide guidance on how to foster the development of self-regulatory skills through play.

The competencies learned through play extend beyond academics, as play is multifaceted. Through play, which allows students to build on complex ideas in sociodramatic play, children develop social and emotional skills. Play supports the development of language as students interact with one another. It also allows young learners to control their impulses as they learn to share and wait their turn during play. The use of play and thematic play centers supports skills involved in the development of self-regulation in classrooms. Play is a platform that fosters linguistic and regulatory skills in Latinx preschools (see Figure 2).

Moreover, developing self-regulation skills in preschool students through the implementation of games can foster these skills in a developmentally appropriate manner. Games that involve movement and oral directions target inhibitory control and conscious control to support academic achievement in Latinx preschool students. It is imperative that activities reinforcing the development of self-regulation are embedded in preschool programs. Therefore, it is proposed that preschool educators implement these activities in classrooms.

Cultural Awareness in the Latinx Preschool Classroom

Another element that can support language development (which consequently fosters cognitive and impulse control) in the Latinx preschool is

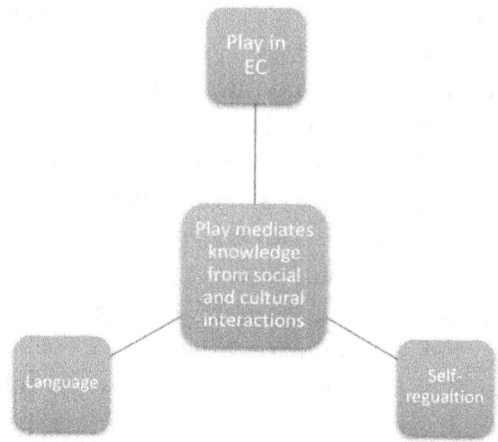

Figure 2. Play as a Mediating Tool Between Language and Self-Regulation

culturally relevant pedagogy. The concept of culturally sensitive or relevant pedagogy is aimed at ensuring that educators use aspects of Latinx culture to support students' overall growth. This pedagogy focuses on several aspects of student achievement and supports while embedding each child's cultural identity. The role of implementing culturally relevant pedagogy is to foster not only critical perspectives but also executive functioning skills. Ladson-Billings (1995) describes three main components of culturally relevant pedagogy: (a) student learning and success, (b) cultural competence to assist, and (c) critical consciousness which refers to the ability to identify, analyze, and challenge societal inequalities. According to this theory, students encountering culturally relevant pedagogy achieve success while maintaining their culture and developing critical consciousness. Culturally relevant pedagogy also embeds the core principle of constructivist pedagogy, that is, it uses students' prior knowledge to engage them, make them active participants, and further their individual learning. Moreover, culturally relevant pedagogy also utilizes what is called "Funds of Knowledge," in which students use their experiences from home, with family and friends, during learning and/or playing in the preschool classroom.

When implementing culturally relevant pedagogy, teachers need to be prepared to be culturally sensitive and receive the required education and training, specifically regarding the values of *educación*, *familismo*, and *respeto* in Latinx children. For example, understanding Latinx families and their values would allow educators to question whether students who are compliant and do not misbehave are learning or understanding. Culturally sensitive educators strive to connect and establish a bond with the Latinx students. It is suggested that that bond then be used to help educators better redirect inappropriate classroom behaviors while helping Latinx students' academic skills.

Assessing Latinx Children

It is critical that early childhood teachers are adequately prepared to observe and assess self-regulatory skills. As important as teacher training is, there is also the issue of finding culturally appropriate assessments that effectively measure such skills in both languages. As previously mentioned, DLLs are developing two languages at the same time, and assessing young learners using one language can lead to erroneous results. Many monolingual tests compared the results to a normative database, or rather a sample, for the population intended. Simply translating an assessment to Spanish is not sufficient for generating reliable results. It is therefore important to have assessment tools that have been standardized for both populations. Even as young learners are developing two languages, they may not necessarily be balanced bilingually. There can be variations of proficiency in either language, especially at such a young age. The level of exposure they have to each language can quickly impact the results of a language assessment. There is variability in language acquisition with respect to time, rate, and sequencing of language that makes assessing DLLs a sensitive phenomenon. While young learners acquire both languages, there are periods of language imbalance. In fact, due to the language imbalance, when a DLL results are compared to monolingual populations, either Spanish or English, they may not perform well in either language. That is because language development happens differently in DLLs and assessment must also be done differently.

Consequently, to successfully distribute bilingual assessments the assessor must also speak both languages. There are variations in the way different Spanish-speaking countries refer to the same thing. For example, many countries refer to corn as maiz, mazorca, elote, choclo, jojoto, or marlo; though all of these words identify the same object, they have varying names depending on the country the child is from. There are several words in the Spanish language where this is common, including instances where accent and pronunciation vary from one Spanish country to the other. There are several Spanish assessments that include one version of the word and children are often marked incorrectly. Thus, having a Spanish-speaking evaluator who is aware of the cultural variations can allow for a more equitable and better representation of the language abilities of young Latinx children.

The present study used PSRA, a field-based measure that was developmentally appropriate for preschoolers. Not only is this tool developmentally appropriate but it is an early childhood tool that is specifically in Spanish and English. Therefore, training teachers and teacher educators to use this measure may increase awareness of the effectiveness of using a developmentally appropriate instrument that allows children to be engaged. The participants in this study enjoyed the battery of tasks presented to them. Children were engaged in the tasks and were eager to play and interact in all activities. The participants were motivated and looked forward to completing each task with the examiner. The battery of PSRA tasks has concurrent validity with other validated measures used to evaluate children's social competence and behavior problems in the early grades. Hence, the PSRA tasks could be used to determine kindergarten placement.

Preparing Teachers to be Multicultural Educators

Many of the recommendations presented above have implications for teacher preparation programs and continuing education. While the term "multiculturalism" is widely used in the United States today, and there is an awareness of the importance of incorporating multicultural practices into the classroom, many still question whether teachers are truly prepared to be multicultural educators in this fast-growing society. Preparation for multicultural education goes beyond educating teachers to simply learn about holidays and celebrate Latinx culture on certain days of the school calendar. Higher educational programs should strive to prepare future educators to become sensitive to different cultures and to develop their lessons and units to reflect the cultures of the students in their classrooms.

In addition, early childhood educators must be trained in teaching academic content in a multicultural, sensitive manner and must become sensitive and able to attend to each culture's needs. According to the U.S. census, data released in 2011, 50.4% of U.S. births were made up of minority children. Thus, teaching and learning in a culturally responsive environment must be implemented, so that specific subcultures do not fall behind. In addition to hiring teachers from culturally responsive early childhood education preparation programs, early childhood education program administrators can make sure to provide workshops on cultural sensitivity and competence in early childhood. In order for minority students to be successful, they need educators who can create a stigma-free, emotionally safe, and supportive early learning environment that has high expectations for all students. This learning environment must be representative of the students in the class in order for all students to succeed by finding culturally responsive and relevant connections between themselves and the subject matter.

Implementing cultural awareness in the classroom also entails increasing Latinx family involvement. Engaging Latinx families requires educators to understand key parental beliefs and goals, specifically, the ways in which *educación*, *familismo*, and *respeto* guide the way in which families fulfill their roles and responsibilities. These values influence parental decisions and behaviors; hence, this understanding would foster Latinx families' engagement.

Engaging Latinx Families in Early Childhood Programs

Despite the differing cultural views and the many barriers to engagement, educators can put forward a set of research-based strategies in order to engage Latinx parents in their young children's education. The next section proposes concrete recommendations for practice, based on the understanding of Latinx cultural values, that can help educators achieve this goal.

Welcoming Families' Cultures into the Classroom

To encourage participation, a program has to create an environment that is inviting and honors the family's presence. Hoover-Dempsey et al., (2005) have found that one of the most important indicators of parental engagement was how welcoming the environment was to the attendees. Some general suggestions for creating a welcoming environment are (a) greeting families at the door, (b) hanging signs in the families' home language so that families can feel welcome and can navigate the building more easily, and (c) establishing a parent-room where parents can mingle (Halgunseth et al., 2009). An environment is welcoming when parents can see their home language and culture represented there. One way of achieving this is by inviting parents to label the classroom in Spanish. Labels can be color-coded so that children can recognize the English and Spanish versions of the words. This practice has a positive effect on parent engagement and on creating an inviting environment for parents and children.

Another way to involve families and cultures is by collecting information about the children at the start of the school year. One activity that many teachers report to be effective at reassuring parents that their culture will be respected while learning about families' cultures and values, is asking parents questions about their children's names. These questions include: (a) What is your child's name? (b) Why did you name them that way? and (c) Does the name have a special meaning? (Tabors & López, 2005). It is recommended that teachers build a book with each child's name, a picture of the child, and a short narrative describing the child's name and meaning in both English and Spanish. Teachers report that this activity gives them an insight into cultural values and practices and can serve as a way of welcoming children, families, and their culture into the classroom. It is also very important that teachers learn to pronounce the child's name appropriately before the year starts, as this makes children and families feel their culture is respected.

Similarly, inviting families to bring cultural artifacts, recipes, and traditional celebrations to the classroom can support the home-school connection. For example, teachers can encourage parents to sing songs and read books in Spanish to the class. In addition, the Spanish language and culture focus on oral interactive narratives as a way of supporting education, and many traditional tales are likely to be transmitted orally rather than through books. Thus, parents can help teachers identify and invite storytellers from the community to tell stories in Spanish (Tabors & López, 2005). It is also important to encourage parents to see the value in continuing to enrich children with the home culture in order to allow engagement and development to continue (Sibley & Dearing, 2014).

Understanding Parents and Being Flexible

In order to best engage Latinx parents, educators need to understand the experiences of immigration. A large number of Latinx parents are immigrants, and the immigration experience and immigration status affect the family's socioeconomic status. In addition, most immigrants have no experience with the American education system. This puts parents at a disadvantage when interacting with educators. Many parents have to work multiple jobs to meet the financial needs of the family; thus, finding the time to become knowledgeable about a new educational system can pose some challenges for them. For these reasons, providing flexible schedules and different opportunities and formats for Latinx parents to participate is indispensable.

It is important to support parents with the time-management aspect of parental engagement by providing information on how to help parents become aware of the functions taking place at school during the academic year and how to request dates for school visits if they cannot come to any set event. Teachers should request feedback on when many events could be held. This allows for more engagement and for the development of a system that depends not only on hearing parents who attend classroom events but also on focusing on those parents who cannot attend. Teachers can plan events by sending letters home in the home language and requesting participation via letters, emails, or phone calls. Furthermore, allowing for a communication method that is multimodal can support the engagement of Latinx parents in early childhood. One effective way of engaging parents to encourage them to visit school centers is to send formal invitations. Latinx values of *educación* and *respeto* dictate that it is not polite to decline such invitations, and when flexibility is provided, most parents will make an effort to attend the event (Mendez Smith & Vega, 2015).

Offering Parenting Classes and Adult Education

Another recommendation for increasing parental engagement in early childhood education programs is to offer parenting classes and adult classes at early learning centers and schools. Such programs provide parents with networking opportunities and valuable knowledge and skills. Programs addressing parenting skills have been shown to be successful at helping parents shift parenting styles, change discipline methods, and improve communication between families and teachers in a group of Latinx immigrant parents. Latinx parents tend to become more engaged in early learning centers and schools when they meet other parents who speak their native language and with whom they feel comfortable (McWayne et al., 2013). Adult classes, especially ones offered in Spanish, can help build groups and friendships among parents, which will in turn enhance parent engagement through the group support formed. One way of ensuring that Latinx parents have the opportunity to build relationships with other parents is by structuring meetings with the idea of supporting parents in supporting one another. Introductory questions and parent activities such as *conocimiento* are effective ways of creating a sense of community among parents (Keyser, 2006). *Conocimiento* can be translated as "knowledge"; in Spanish, however, it means "working knowledge." This activity is structured as a series of posters with a question at the top of each poster. Parents have felt markers, use them to write their ideas on each poster, and work together to share their working and life knowledge with each other. Some sample questions are: What are your child's strengths? What are your family's strengths? What do you hope your children will learn in this program? What are some questions you have about children? What do you like to do for fun? What are some of the most enjoyable things you do with your children? (Keyser, 2006). This activity can encourage parents to share ideas, build relationships and become more involved in their child's education.

Conducting Home Visits

Home visits are a hallmark of Head Start, Early Head Start, and many other early childhood education programs. Home visits can provide educators with a better understanding of the home environment, family dynamics, and culture, as they provide an informal way to connect with parents in a manner that might feel less threatening and more comfortable. Home visits can prevent communication problems or help resolve them in an efficient manner. Research shows that when kindergarten teachers conducted home visits, there have been improved relationships with families and children as well as stronger parent-teacher communication. Similarly, home visits were related to student improvements in literacy skills, math skills, and children's participation in class activities.

Latinx parents typically respond very well to home visits because of the value of *familismo* and the idea that the home and the family are the centers of the child's life, and thus important decisions should be made in the home. In addition, when educators come to the home, they are showing respect for the role of the family and for the family's culture.

Sharing the Decision-Making Process

Shared decision-making is a very important and often overlooked part of parental engagement. Head Start programs encourage families to be integral parts of decision-making and to participate in leadership roles. This shows families that their opinions are valued and that they have an ownership stake in the program. Some centers make it a point to consult with parents in the hiring of new staff and in the selection of services and activities that the center provides (Halgunseth & Peterson, 2009). Nevertheless, Flaugher (2006) found that despite the awareness of the importance of sharing decision-making power with parents, in actuality, the opportunities for decision-making are limited, and minority families are the least likely to feel that the decision-making power is shared.

Encouraging Latinx parents to share in the decision-making process regarding programs or curricula might be a challenge for most educators because of the parents' value of *respeto* and deference to educators and professionals. Nevertheless, one way to start is by asking parents about their priorities and goals in the education process, as well as their child's strengths and interests. It is helpful for educators to encourage parents to make decisions as a group and communicate those decisions with the center. The ability to make the decisions with a group can help Latinx parents overcome their fear of violating the value of *respeto*.

Conclusion

This study began with two personal stories that led to the realization that current kindergarten programs do not focus on self-regulation skills. With current educational policies focusing on standardized testing as a measure of academic development, earlier grades introduce academics earlier on, not allowing for focus on skills such as self-regulation that foster academic development. This study ends with a discussion based on findings relating to impulse and cognitive control between language and self-regulation in Latinx DLLs.

This study intended to reveal that skills such as self-regulation, which are not taught but are needed in schools, have associations with academics. Overall, the findings of this study support the notion that self-regulation is tied to language and literacy as reported by statistically significant correlations. This investigation also revealed positive correlations between language and self-regulation in DLLs. Suggestions for additional research have been described that could help look at the vast and recently discussed issue of self-regulation and overall preschool development.

Self-regulation constitutes the child's ability to successfully manage emotional and cognitive states during stressful or demanding situations and to engage in successful interactions with peers and adults. As children develop, they need to find a balance between their ability to exhibit self-regulation and their desire for self-assertion. The ability to control emotions and behaviors enables a student to perform well on tasks. Self-regulatory skills had been associated with language, social and cognitive skills. In contrast, a lack of self-regulatory skills is linked to behavioral problems in preschool children. Children with a low level of self-regulation tend to deal poorly with change and have higher levels of anxiety and stress. Preschool students who lack strong behavioral self-regulation skills have difficulty performing in classrooms with set curricula and agendas. Furthermore, children with low levels of inhibitory control have difficulty paying attention in class. Impulsive behavior limits their ability to hold on to new information taught in classrooms and leads them to become unsuccessful students when tested in a formal school setting.

Despite the centrality of self-regulatory skills, Latinx preschoolers were shown to develop regulatory skills at a slower rate than English-language proficient preschoolers. As the Latinx population continues to grow, it is imperative to examine the relationship between language and self-regulation among Latinx preschoolers for application to policy and curriculum development (Castro et al., 2013). The lack of policies and access to quality early childhood programs that support Latinx young learners puts them at a greater academic disadvantage than that faced by their white peers. Since early childhood programs are guided by a system that emphasizes test-driven curricula resulting from current educational policies, Latinx preschoolers face significant academic challenges that do not address their needs (Castro et al., 2013). Latinx preschoolers need to have programs that address non-cognitive aspects of development while skillfully supporting academics such as literacy and language development. This is particularly the case because language is a key factor in the ability to self-regulate, an ability that then inherently leads to academic gains.

Some areas of priority to support Latinx children are focusing on language development, child-teacher interactions, and classroom quality that supports the positive social development of the Latinx preschool student. Language proficiency is an indicator of social and emotional competencies. Lack of communication and expression, as well as lack of understanding of verbal direction, instruction, or classroom talk, can lead to negative socio-emotional development in young children.

It is important to focus on Latinx students' interactions with teachers in order to ensure children understand the cultural context and social interactions that are happening. Therefore, it is desirable to reduce classroom sizes, as that promotes greater teacher-student interaction and individualized education (Ferjan Ramirez & Kuhl, 2017). In addition, teachers need to maintain and encourage a positive social environment among Latinx preschoolers and support their relationships with all their peers and teachers in the classroom.

The implementation of play can allow for the development of several skills at once, specifically: language, social interactions, impulse, and behavioral control. Latinx students need schools to design strategies to support active transport and increase student physical activity, such as outdoor learning, throughout the school day. Incorporating outdoor and indoor play can support Latinx students' developmental domains, as play supports the development of language as students interact with one another. It also allows young learners to control their impulses as they learn to share and wait their turn during play. The use of play and thematic play centers supports skills involved in the development of self-regulation in classrooms.

Another element that can support language development (which consequently fosters cognitive and impulse control) in the Latinx preschool is culturally relevant pedagogy. When implementing culturally relevant pedagogy, teachers need to be prepared to be culturally sensitive and receive the required education and training, specifically regarding the values of *educación*, *familismo*, and *respeto* in Latinx children. Implementing cultural awareness in the classroom also entails increasing Latinx family involvement. Engaging Latinx families requires educators to understand key parental beliefs and goals, specifically, the ways in which *educación*, *familismo*, and *respeto* guide the way in which families fulfill their roles and responsibilities. Despite the differing cultural views and the many barriers to engagement, educators can put forward a set of research-based strategies in order to engage Latinx parents in their young children's education. Some ways of achieving that goal are by welcoming families' culture into the classroom and creating an environment that is inviting and honors the family's presence.

Another recommendation for increasing parental engagement in early childhood education programs is to offer parenting classes and adult classes at early learning centers and schools. Latinx parents tend to become more engaged in early learning centers and schools when they meet other parents who speak their native language and with whom they feel comfortable (McWayne et al., 2013). Furthermore, conducting home visits can provide educators with a better understanding of the home environment, family dynamics, and culture, as they provide an informal way to connect with parents in a manner that might feel less threatening and more comfortable. Last, by sharing the decision-making process, educators ensure that families' opinions are valued and that families have an ownership stake in the program.

· 6 ·

LESSONS LEARNED

By Claritz Marte, Laura Giolitti Egui, and Margaret Calabro

This book began with two personal vignettes that shared how this research started. Fittingly, this book concludes with a compilation of personal narratives of our former students who are educators and who have embedded self-regulatory practices in their educational pedagogies. As a result of the continued paucity of research and expertise that exist with regard to self-regulation among the Latinx DLL community, we collect the following narratives from educators with expertise in different areas that collectively give a voice to the topic of the development of self-regulation skills in Latinx DLLs. Their expertise ranges from knowledge in early childhood, bilingual education, special education, and support services, to early childhood higher education teacher preparation.

The first vignette is written by Claritz Marte, a Latinx early childhood educator (ECE) who is also a fierce advocate for equitable practice for Latinx children in the public school system. Claritz has embedded play activities to support her students and her son's self-assertion, communication skills, and self-regulation in her pedagogical practices. The second vignette is by Laura Giolitti Egui, a Latinx and bilingual early childhood special education specialist who provides services to children and their families with learning needs. The final vignette is written by Margaret Calabro who prepares pre-service teachers in the early childhood and early intervention fields and implements a blended curricular approach to provide comprehensive support and services for young children, and their families.

Lessons Learned by ECE Bilingual Educator Claritz Marte

Fellowship is a form of unification created through the connection between communalities in any society. However, when people have differences and there is a lack of communication, the possibility of fellowship bounding reduces. Fortunately, authors and educators Ruth Guirguis and Raquel Plotka have brought several solutions in their book, *The Development of Self-Regulation in Latinx Preschool Children*, for educators and parents to build upon Latinx children's self-regulation, language skills, and academic achievement. Educators must practice culturally responsive pedagogy, and Latinx parents must change parents' strategies by working collaboratively as colleagues with their respective students' teachers to achieve quality education for Latinx children. As an overall takeaway from this lecture, I have learned the importance of self-regulation and language in correlation with academic success and the practices I can implement as a teacher and Latinx mother of two.

The importance of self-regulation in preschoolers is critical. According to the authors, self-regulation in children is the control of impulses, emotions, and behaviors which improve their overall development, socio-emotional and linguistic skills, as well as their academic learning. Socially and emotionally, children can positively interact with peers and teachers while learning; "Once preschool children have developed emotionally and behaviorally, the ability to achieve social competence and peer acceptance emerge." Moreover, through self-regulation, children can improve language, especially "inner speech," and internalize information according to the Vygotskian framework. After this internalization of information occurs, emotions and behaviors are more easily controlled by preschoolers, and their likelihood for improvement in attention, vocabulary, and memory automatically results in increased academic achievements. Self-regulation in Latinx children is essential for their overall development and academic achievement. Therefore, politicians, educators, and parents should consider following the subsequent actions to improve these children's quality of life and education.

The first actions I will take as a professional in the Early Childhood Education setting are remembering the Latinx parents' cultural barriers and following culturally responsive pedagogy. The authors explain cultural barriers in the Latinx community in parents' participation in their children's education. These are, *educación*, social manners implied to children according to people's age and authority; *familismo*, the importance of interpersonal relationships and decisions making within the family, and *respeto*, mutual respect between authoritarians, parents holding authority at home, and teachers at school. By remembering these cultural aspects of the Latinx community, I will be able to facilitate my practices of culturally responsive teaching in my classroom. For instance, in the Latinx community, children are taught not to question adults; I will do my best as a bilingual teacher to build on this knowledge, support them to develop confidence and autonomy, and improve their self-regulation through constant communication.

Additionally, to foster the concept of *familismo*, I will create a welcoming bilingual environment for Latinx parents through workshops through *conocimiento* (working knowledge) to improve their knowledge of the American educational system and construct their participation in their children's education. Last, I will collaborate with Latinx parents in all educational decisions to enhance their children's education by asking about aspects of their culture (such as the origin of their child's name), participating in cultural classroom activities, and using "Funds of Knowledge" from their community in the children's learning. As a professional educator, I will connect with Latinx parents and children in a culturally respectful manner. In that case, I will be able to build positive learning experiences for their children and improve the possibility of self-regulation and quality learning in the classroom.

Second, as a mother of a Latinx preschooler, I will remember and continue to put into practice the importance of proper disciplining and communication style with my son, so I can improve self-regulation before he enters kindergarten. As a Latinx mother, it was emotionally complex for me to read that Latinx mothers use "controlling" and physical strategies for disciplining their children as a result of cultural aspects. When my older son (now 10 years old) was a preschooler, I used to be very stern, controlling him for not paying attention or learning the lessons provided by his homework. Unfortunately, this led to worsening self-regulatory skills at school, and the teachers often called me to come and pick him up early. My son suffered from a lack of interpersonal relationships with his teachers and me, his primary caregiver. My educational background has provided me with a better comprehension of children's development, behaviors, and emotional responses; my younger toddler will benefit from having me as a mother. Since communication, positive reinforcement, and self-regulation are tied positively, my discipline style has drastically improved, and I do playful activities. Specifically, reading books, singing, dancing, and eye-to-eye, soft-toned conversations with my children to improve their self-regulatory and linguistic skills; it is working exceptionally well.

As constructivists of society, we teachers are responsible for connecting as fellow students with all communities integrated into our classrooms. The Latinx community is one of the fastest-growing immigrant communities in the United States. Consequently, it is the teachers' role to develop their knowledge of the overall/individual cultures within the Latinx community better to develop culturally responsive teaching to their students and connect with their parents as fellows with the same purpose of improving quality education for the students. Additionally, many Latinx parents and I will benefit from reading *The Development of Self-Regulation in Latinx Preschool Children* because it brings up how negative reinforcement of discipline is ineffective in children's development. Finally, in hopes of improving self-regulation, more vital communication skills, and academic success in Latinx children, this framework falls into the right hand of politicians, educators, and parents who desire to improve quality education for all Latinx children.

Lessons Learned by ECE Bilingual Intervention Specialist Laura Giolitti Egui

As a Venezuelan education specialist who has worked with different groups of students for more than 16 years, I can affirm that self-regulation is a key component for healthy development and successful school life to occur. I have taught children of different ages, social economic statuses, and cultural backgrounds, in different languages, and even in different countries. Across all the children that have been under my care, I noticed that providing constant opportunities for the children to practice their self-regulation skills is necessary for their functional performance in and out of school. For this to be possible, it is imperative that teachers can provide a safe environment for them to explore different ways to self-regulate as well as the appropriate tools to support them throughout the process with compassion, empathy, and knowledge.

When referring to knowledge, I refer to the need of being knowledgeable of the different factors that can have an impact on the way the child develops depending on their age, race, cultural background, socioeconomic status, or any type of special need. New York is one of the cities in which the population is more varied and diverse. A significant percentage of its population is Latinx. Being Latinx does not only mean that you grow up surrounded by people who speak Spanish, but it also involves other cultures, manners, behavioral expectations, and social norms. Therefore, the challenges that the children of this community have (especially while growing up in a country that does not share necessarily the same core values, educational system, and language) are greater than they are for most of the North American population.

Understanding emotions is complex for any human being at any age, especially during their childhood years. It is then that educational systems need to guide children in a way where they can grow up feeling understood, capable, and confident. Self-regulation requires being knowledgeable of specific language related to the emotions we feel and how we can express our needs, thoughts, and wants to others. Imagine how it would feel to grow up in a culture that perceives emotions differently than yours does, that uses words associated with them that are not part of your own language, and that has social expectations different than those you have at home. It must be a great challenge.

Dr. Plotka and Dr. Guirguis had written this wonderful piece in which they advocate for Latinx children and their families. The way they have outlined each of the chapters and their content is admirable, especially by highlighting three main core values of any Latinx community such as *respeto*, *familismo*, and *educación* right from the first chapter. Not everyone can understand how these can impact the way you behave, the way you perceive the world, and the way your own core values are developed later in life. It is common to see how Latinx parents tend to force their acquisition of North American society's values by putting aside their own just to try to fit in the system. As a consequence, there is a disconnection between the new generation's home culture and their adopted one, as well as great difficulties in building a strong self-identity. In order to provide an inclusive and respectful learning environment for the Latinx communities in this country, it is absolutely necessary to navigate and deeply understand the meaning of these core values. This is necessary in order to successfully align said core values with the different options of curricula available in our preschools as a way to advocate for the maintenance and enrichment of Latinx cultural background.

Furthermore, later in the book, the authors highlight some important educational components that are closely interrelated with the ability to self-regulate appropriately. Most people might think that being able to self-regulate is just a matter of following the rules, tolerating boundaries, and using coping skills. As the authors demonstrate, self-regulation involves much more than that. Developing strong self-regulation skills will have a positive impact on the academic achievement and proper functioning of any human being. In my opinion, this book should be shared with any person involved in the educational field. It is the perfect combination of the key components that help us to understand the past, present, and future projections of how we can enhance the developmental opportunities for our communities of Latinx children and their families. In this way, we will ensure a future population with high academic achievement, strong self-identity, and healthy socio-emotional development.

Lessons Learned by ECE Higher Education Instructor Margaret Calabro

I recall looking around my classroom and a wave of anxiety washing over me. It was my first day teaching a class of Pre-K students and the stress of the responsibility weighed heavily on my shoulders. While I was armed with knowledge from my studies and observations, I struggled to quiet my troubling thoughts. Worrisome scenarios raced through my mind as my hands began to slightly shake. I glanced out of the window and noticed school buses were arriving. I took two deep breaths, shook out my trembling hands, and walked down the hallway to greet my new students with a wide smile across my face. It was soon that I realized the only way to teach my students the crucial skill of self-regulation was to model the behavior myself. Controlling my own anxiety and emotions would be a key component to success for the children in my class. I also recognized the significant toll a lack of self-regulation has on a child's behavior.

Throughout my years as an early childhood educator, I consistently witnessed children struggle with the ability to understand their emotions. Violent behavior and impulsivity became reoccurring aspects of the school day, as many children were overwhelmed with frustration. This included a long list of students who were labeled as "emotionally disturbed" and later placed in smaller, more restrictive kindergarten settings. At the end of each school year, I could not help but think, "I failed some of these children. I should have been more prepared. I should have done more."

As a pre-service teacher educator, I have come to implement strategies that I learned during my teaching years and in many of the courses I took. While professional development training and educational philosophies have provided reliable and proven approaches to ensure a child's ability to self-regulate, there is still so much that needs to be taught in teacher preparation programs. In my lectures, I teach pre-service teachers through hands-on activities and incorporate plenty of movement and focus on social and emotional learning. Intentional preparation and modeling self-regulatory skills can better prepare ECE teachers.

Nonetheless, the reality is that teaching young children to self-regulate is a challenging task considering the current nature of modern-day classrooms. Resources and materials are often limited. There is typically little tolerance from the administration for straying from the daily schedule. While play is incorporated, the children remain in one small room for the majority of their school day and outdoor play is not always guaranteed. The school day tends to feel rushed as the day is split into periods, only allowing so much time for each activity. Naturally, teachers become overwhelmed with the pressure of standards expectations, which leads to them struggling to manage their own emotional wellness. At times it feels as though the entire school system is working against ECE teachers. What can prepare new teachers for this reality?

Reflecting on the book by authors Dr. Guirguis and Dr. Plotka, I believe that the recommendations of implementing play and language as well as fostering parental engagement are key aspects in the process of supporting regulatory skills. Their recommendations align with my personal educational experiences where students responded most to my support when I validated their feelings, allowed students a few minutes to stop for a break, and modeled prosocial behaviors. Self-regulation is a skill even adults spend significant time developing. The best we can do for our young students and our pre-service early childhood education teachers is to teach them strategies, such as those mentioned by the authors, that will help lay the foundation for a life of emotional, behavioral, and cognitive control.

AFTERWORD

SELF-REGULATION AND COVID-19

The research that was conducted looking at Latinx children was conducted during a typical academic year. Consequently, it is important to note that this data was collected and analyzed prior to the COVID-19 pandemic. The results suggest that we have been failing Latinx young learners as they develop both their language and self-regulatory skills. There has also been a lack of focus on Latinx students and their executive skills. This research comes at a critical time as we now are entering a post-pandemic educational era and there still exists a paucity of research that specifically focuses on the support and curricula needed to foster the development of self-regulation in Latinx children. Additionally, this research can be used as early childhood teachers are now faced with incoming students who lived through the COVID-19 pandemic, whose schooling came to a complete halt in 2020, and who have fallen behind in the development of skills such as cognitive regulation and impulse control.

After schools were closed down due to the COVID-19 pandemic in 2020, children were forced to continue their education through asynchronous or synchronous formats. While this was challenging for students of all ages, it was particularly challenging for young learners. Young learners were faced with having to learn through online platforms, no longer socialize with their peers or teachers, and could not return to the classrooms they once had played and learned in. Many young learners watched as their families were impacted by the effects of being in a global lockdown. For young learners who lived in lower socioeconomic areas, the challenges were far more severe. The COVID-19 pandemic had a harsher impact on students of color who lived in multi-generational homes. Latinx young children were greatly affected as many preschools and/or headstarts that exist in less affluent areas did not have the technology to offer families a continued curriculum at home. Many Latinx families also did not have the privilege of being part of schools that created learning pods for young learners as in affluent areas. Learning pods allowed one family to supervise a group of young learners and alternative supervisory duties with other families. The children remained together and attended school virtually as a small group while always having one adult to support and scaffold activities at home. This was not an opportunity that many underserved communities had as housing, job, and food insecurities existed along with language and technological barriers. These aspects combined created a prolonged traumatic experience for many Latinx DLLs who missed months of schooling.

Trauma can affect self-regulatory skills. Trauma can range from acute to chronic experiences, and from short and long-term experiences. Specifically during COVID-19 young children experienced isolation and in some instances, lost members of their families, as well as experienced housing insecurities. The trauma of isolation affects both the social and cognitive domains of development among preschoolers, creating a greater risk of trauma in young children and having negative results on both cognitive and impulse control. Traumatic experiences can trigger inappropriate behaviors and responses in children. Children react and regulate differently when they have been through a prolonged period of trauma, or, as with COVID-19, long periods of isolation. Typically, self-regulation can be facilitated in the classroom through intentional pedagogical strategies and approaches. Cognitive regulation can also be fostered in the classroom by providing young learners with mindfulness opportunities. Mindfulness activities in young learners foster behaviors such as paying attention, as well as the recognition and subsequent identification of feelings. . . . Early childhood educators support these skills by modeling appropriate social behaviors and scaffolding impulse and cognitive skills.

How the pandemic exacerbated this existing issue in young Latinx children is yet to be determined. The missed school days and low enrollment in early childhood programs translated to missed learning opportunities. Due to school closures, social distancing policies, and isolation protocols, students lost routines, peer relationships, and social interactions that support language development. Classroom activities such as sociodramatic play, which helps students with expressive skills and impulse control, were not allowed when schools began to re-open. Students were encouraged not to share and to not talk to one another to prevent the spread of the COVID-19 virus. Skills such as listening to others speak and waiting your turn to speak, which is a form of regulation, disappeared during the COVID-19 pandemic. Children, for safety reasons, were not only discouraged from talking and having conversations with each other but were physically separated. Young learners sat in classrooms in individual seats rather than in small or large group settings, wore masks, had plastic dividers that created physical barriers between peers and from the teacher, and were not to approach each other or the teacher. While young learners went back to their classrooms, social integration was simply not allowed. This was the way many young learners were introduced to the concept of school and learning. This was the way it was for the next academic year.

Cognitive regulation was also impacted. The attention span that children had on activities during online learning drastically decreased. Young learners are sensory learners and use their senses to gather information. Online learning is limited to only two senses, specifically auditory and visual learning. Students with learning differences struggled in these formats, and the long-term results of this are still unknown. What does this mean for students with learning loss as they re-enter schools again? What support services will be needed to close the learning gap of these disruptions? What does this mean for Latinx students already facing regulatory disparities in their preschool programs? Are current educators being provided with the resources to support these students and their families better?

Self-regulation, such as impulse control, is aligned with emotional development, while cognitive control is aligned with attentional and behavioral development. Online learning requires the ability of individuals to manage their own learning. In young children, the ability of students to learn to avoid distraction and focus on a task has not been achieved. Organizational skills are often monitored by the adults around young children until these skills through routines are learned. During COVID-19, young learners missed out on this type of learning needed for later academic years. While these are skills that can be taught, the academic focus at an earlier age will make this process of making up for lost skills more challenging. Now more than ever, as we enter post-pandemic learning, there needs to be a conscious and intentional focus on supporting Latinx children's self-regulatory skills.

APPENDIX A

Home Language Questionnaire (HLQ) English
Dear Parent or Person in Parental Relation:
In order to provide your child with the best possible education, we need to determine how well he or she understands, speaks, reads, and writes in English, as well as prior school and personal history. Please complete the sections below entitled Language Background and Educational History. Your assistance in answering these questions is greatly appreciated.
Thank you.

APPENDIX A

STUDENT NAME:			
First	*Middle*	*Last*	

DATE OF BIRTH:			GENDER:
			Male
Month	*Day*	*Year*	Female

PARENT/PERSON IN PARENTAL		RELATION INFO:	
Last Name		*First Name*	*Relation to*

Language Background (Please check all that apply.)			
1. What language(s) is(are) spoken in the student's home or residence?	English	Other	
2. What was the first language your child learned?	English	Other	
3. What is the Home Language of each parent/guardian?	Parent 1 Guardian(s)	Parent 2	
4. What language(s) does your child understand?	English	Other	
5. What language(s) does your child speak?	English	Other	Does not speak
6. What language(s) does your child read?	English	Other	Does not read
7. What language(s) does your child write?	English	Other	Does not write

Educational History
8. Indicate the total number of years that your child has been enrolled in school
9. Do you think your child may have any difficulties or conditions that affect his or her ability to understand, speak, read, or write in English or any other language? If yes, please describe them. Yes* No Not sure 　　　　　　　*If yes, please explain: How severe do you think these difficulties are? Minor   Somewhat severe   Very severe
10a. Has your child ever been <u>referred</u> for a special education evaluation in the past? No   Yes* *Please complete 10b below
10b. *<u>If referred for an evaluation,</u> has your child ever <u>received</u> any special education services in the past? 　　q No Yes—Type of services received: Age at which services received (Please check all that apply): 　　q Birth to 3 years (Early Intervention) 3 to 5 years (Special Education) 6 years or older (Special Education) 10c. Does your child have an Individualized Education Program (IEP)?   No   Yes
11. Is there anything else you think is important for the school to know about your child? (e.g., special talents, health concerns, etc.)
12. In what language(s) would you like to receive information from the school?

Cuestionario de Idioma del Hogar ("HLQ" por sus siglas en inglés)
Estimados padres o tutores:
Con el fin de proporcionar la mejor educación posible a su hijo(a), necesitamos determinar el nivel del habla, lectura, escritura y comprensión en el inglés, así como conocer su educación previa e historial personal. Por favor, llene con su información las secciones "Conocimientos de idiomas" e "Historial educativo." Apreciamos mucho su colaboración respondiendo a estas preguntas. Gracias.

Por favor escriba con claridad al completar esta sección.
NOMBRE DEL ESTUDIANTE:
Nombre   Segundo   Apellido
nombre
FECHA DE NACIMIENTO:	**GÉNERO:**
	❏ Masculino
Mes Día Año	❏ Femenino
INFORMACIÓN DE LOS PADRES / PERSONA EN RELACIÓN PARENTAL	
Apellido Primer Nombre Relación con el estudiante	

| Conocimientos de idiomas |
(Por favor, marque todas las opciones que sean aplicables)
1. ¿Qué idioma(s) se habla(n) en el hogar o residencia del estudiante?   ❏ Inglés   ❏ Otro
2. ¿Cuál fue el primer idioma que su hijo(a) aprendió?   ❏ Inglés   ❏ Otro
3. ¿Cuál es el idioma primario de cada padre / tutor?   ❏ Madre   ❏ Padre
❏ Tutor(es)

4. ¿Qué idioma o idiomas entiende su hijo(a)?	❏ Inglés	❏ Otro	
5. ¿Qué idioma o idiomas habla su hijo(a)?	❏ Inglés	❏ Otro	❏ No sabe hablar
6. ¿Qué idioma o idiomas lee su hijo(a)?	❏ Inglés	❏ Otro	❏ No sabe leer
7. ¿Qué idioma o idiomas escribe su hijo(a)?	❏ Inglés	❏ Otro	❏ No sabe escribir

Historial Educativo
8. Indique con un número el total de años que su hijo(a) lleva inscrito en una escuela:
9. ¿Cree usted que su hijo(a) pueda tener dificultades, interferencias o problemas educacionales que le afecten su capacidad para entender, hablar, leer o escribir en inglés o en cualquier otro idioma? En caso afirmativo, por favor descríbalos. Sí*   No   No se sabe ❏   ❏   ❏ * En caso afirmativo, por favor explique: ¿Qué gravedad considera usted que tienen estas dificultades educacionales? ❏ Poca gravedad ❏ Algo grave ❏ Muy grave

10a. ¿Alguna vez se ha recomendado a su hijo(a) a tener una evaluación de educación especial? ❑ No ❑ Sí* * Por favor, llene 10b. 10b. *<u>Si se le ha recomendado alguna vez una evaluación,</u> ¿ha <u>recibido</u> su hijo(a) alguna vez alguna forma de educación especial? ❑ No ❑ Sí—Explique, que forma o formas de educación especial recibió:
Edad en la que recibió la intervención o forma de educación especial (favor de marcar todas las opciones que sean aplicables): ❑ De nacimiento a 3 años (Intervención Temprana) ❑ 3 a 5 años (Educación Especial) ❑ 6 años o mayor (Educación Especial) 10c. ¿Tiene su hijo(a) un Programa de Educación Individualizada ("IEP" por sus siglas en inglés)? ❑ No ❑ Sí
11. ¿Considera que hay alguna otra información importante que la escuela deba saber sobre su hijo(a)? (Por ejemplo, talentos especiales, problemas de salud, etc.)
12. ¿En qué idioma(s) quiere usted recibir la información de la escuela?

Sequential Second Language Acquisition Assessment Tool

The second language acquisition survey instrument for young learners is to be completed by the classroom/head teacher

STAGE 1—Home language use—Child uses only Spanish.

STAGE 2—Nonverbal—Child communicates with gestures and actions.

STAGE 3—Telegraphic and Formulaic Speech—Child communicates using one or two words.

STAGE 4—Productive Language—Child understands most of what is said in classroom. He/She speaks in longer phrases and complete sentences. There are frequent word errors.

STAGE 5—Fluent English User—Child speaks English in most social and learning. contexts. Language in content areas is still challenging.

APPENDIX B

Dear Parents/Guardians

We are in the process of conducting research on preschool children's behavior management and language skills. This research has been approved by Wyandanch Union Free School District's Board of Education.

As part of this study, the children will be tested twice on their reading, language, and behavior management skills. Testing will take place in November and at the end of the year. The children will be assessed during school hours and there will be no interference in classroom routines or risks to have your child participate in this study. Some of the information will be used for my paper. All names and information will be kept confidential. Participation in this study is voluntary and you may withdraw your child at any time.

Please feel free to contact me if you have any questions or require additional information: Ruth Guirguis: rguirguis@gmail.com

Sincerely,
Ruth Guirguis
Please sign and return this permission form to your child's teacher and keep the top form for your records.

_____ I have read the letter about the behavior and literacy skills study and give consent for my child to participate in the study.

_____
Signature of Parent/Guardian

_____   _____
Name of Child   Date

Estimados Padres/Guardián

Estamos en el proceso de realizar una investigación sobre el manejo del comportamiento y las habilidades lingüísticas de los niños en edad preescolar. Esta investigación ha sido aprobada por la Junta de Educación del Distrito Escolar Libre de Wyandanch Union.

Como parte de este estudio, los niños serán evaluados dos veces en sus habilidades de lectura, lenguaje y manejo del comportamiento. Las pruebas se llevarán a cabo en noviembre y al final del año. Los niños serán evaluados durante el horario escolar y no habrá interferencia en las rutinas del salón de clases ni riesgos para que su hijo participe en este estudio. Parte de la información se utilizará para mi artículo. Todos los nombres y la información se mantendrán confidenciales. La participación en este estudio es voluntaria y puede retirar a su hijo en cualquier momento.

No dude en ponerse en contacto conmigo si tiene alguna pregunta o necesita información adicional: Ruth Guirguis: rguirguis@gmail.com

Atentamente,
Ruth Guirguis

Por favor firme y retorne este formulario a su maestra(o). Mantenga la porción de arriba para su información.

_____   _____
_____ He leído la carta sobre conducta y habilidades en lectura y doy permiso para que mi hijo(a) participe en el estudio.

_____
Firma de Padre/Guardián

_____   _____
Nombre de su hijo   (a) Fecha

REFERENCES

Arslan, E., Durmusoglu-Saltali, N., & Yilmaz, H. (2011). Social skills and emotional and behavioral traits of preschool children. *Social Behavior and Personality, 39*(9), 1281–1288. doi:10.2224/sbp.2011.39.9.1281

Bierman, K. L., Domitrovich, C. E., Nix, R. L., Gest, S. D., Welsh, J. A., Greenberg, M. T., & Gill, S. (2008). Promoting academic and social-emotional school readiness: The Head Start REDI program. *Child Development, 79*(6), 1802–1817. doi:10.1111/j.1467-8624.2008.01227.x

Blair, C. (2002). School readiness: Integrating cognition and emotion in a neurobiological conceptualization of children's functioning at school entry. *American Psychologist, 57*(2), doi:10.1037/0003-066X.57.2.111

Blair, C., & Razza, R. (2007). Relating effortful control, executive function, and false belief understanding to emerging math and literacy ability in kindergarten. *Child Development, 78*(2), 647–663. doi:10.1111/j.1467-8624.2007.01019.x

Bodrova, E., & Leong, D. (2008). Developing self-regulation in kindergarten: Can we keep all the crickets in the basket? *Young Children, 63,* 56–58.

Bronson, M. B. (2000). *Self-regulation in early childhood.* New York, NY: Guilford.

Cameron, C. E., & Morrison, F. J. (2011). Teacher activity orienting predicts preschooler's academic and self-regulatory skills. *Early Education & Development, 22,* 620–648. doi:10.1080/10409280903544405

REFERENCES

Castro, D. C., Garcia, E. E., & Markos, A. M. (2013). *Dual language learners: Research informing policy*. Chapel Hill: The University of North Carolina, Frank Porter Graham Child Development Institute, Center for Early Care and Education-Dual Language Learner.

Chang, F., Crawford, G., Early, D., Bryant, D., Howes, C., Burchinal, M., Barbarin, O., Clifford, R., & Pianta, R. (2007). Spanish-speaking children's social and language development in pre-kindergarten classrooms. *Early Education and Development, 18*(2), 243–269. doi:10.1080/10409280701282959

Cohen, L. E. (2008). Foucault and the early childhood classroom. *Educational Studies, 44*, 7–21. doi:10.1080/00131940802224948

Cole, P. M., Dennis, T. A., Smith-Simon, K. E., & Cohen, L. H. (2009). Preschoolers' emotion regulation strategy understanding: Relations with emotion socialization and child self-regulation. *Social Development, 18*(2), 324–352. doi:10.1111/j.1467-9507.2088.00503.x

Crockenberg, S., & Litman, C. (1990). Autonomy as competence in 2-year-olds: Maternal correlates of child defiance, compliance, and self-assertion. *Developmental Psychology, 26*(6), 961–971. doi:10.1037/0012-1649.26.6.961

Day, K. L., & Smith, C. L. (2013). Understanding the role of private speech in children's emotion regulation. *Early Childhood Research Quarterly, 28*, 405–414. doi:10.1016/j.ecresq.2012.10.003

Delgado-Gaitan, C. (2004). *Involving Latino families in schools: Raising student achievement through home-school partnerships*. Thousand Oaks, CA: Corwin Press.

Denham, S. A., Bassett, H. H., Mincic, M., Kalb, S., Way, E., Wyatt, T., & Segal, Y. (2012a). Social-emotional learning profiles of preschoolers' early school success: A person-centered approach. *Learning and Individual Differences, 22*, 178–189. doi:10.1016/j.lindif.2011.05.001

Denham, S. A., Bassett, H. H., Way, E., Mincic, M., Zinsser, K., & Graling, K. (2012b). Preschoolers' emotion knowledge: Self-regulatory foundations, and predictions of early school success. *Cognition and Emotion, 26*(4), 667–670. doi:10.1080/02699931.2011.602049

DesRosiers, F. S. (1998). *The role of the family and culture on Toddler's developing self-concept: A focus on pride and shame, autonomy, and compliance* (Dissertation). Fordham University, New York, NY.

Diamond, A., Barnett, W. S., Thomas, J., & Munro, S. (2007). Online supplemental material for preschool program improves cognitive control. *Science, 318*, 1–24. doi:10.1126/science.1151148

Diamond, A., & Taylor, C. (1996). Development of an aspect of executive control: Development of the abilities to remember what I said and to "do as I say, not as I do." *Developmental Psychobiology, 29*(4), 315–334.

Diemer, M. C., Treviño, M. S., & Gerstein, E. D. (2021). Contextualizing the role of intrusive parenting in toddler behavior problems and emotion regulation: Is more always worse? *Developmental Psychology, 57*(8), 1242–1253. https://doi.org/10.1037/dev0001231.

Dix, T., Stewart, A. D., Gershoff, E. T., & Day, W. H. (2007). Autonomy and children's reactions to being controlled: Evidence that both compliance and defiance may be positive markers in early development. *Child Development, 78*(4), 1204–1221. doi:10.1111/j.1467-8624.2007.01061.x

REFERENCES

Domitrovich, C. E., Cortes, R. C., & Greenberg, M. T. (2007). Improving young children's social and emotional competence: A randomized trial of the preschool "paths" curriculum. *The Journal of Primary Prevention, 28*(2). 67–91. doi:10.1007/s10935-007-0081-0

Elias, C. L., & Berk, L. E. (2002). Self-regulation in young children: Is there a role for sociodramatic play? *Early Childhood Research Quarterly, 17,* 216–238.

Epstein, S., Pacini, R., Denes-Raj, V., & Heier, H. (1996). Individual differences in intuitive–experiential and analytical–rational thinking styles. *Journal of Personality and Social Psychology, 71*(2), 390–405. doi:10.1037/0022-3514.71.2.390

Farver, J. M., Nakamoto, J., & Lonigan, C. (2007). Assessing preschoolers' emergent literacy skills in English and Spanish with Get Ready to Read! Screening tool. *The International Dyslexia Association, 57,* 161–178. doi:10.10007/s11881-007-00007-9

Feldman, R., & Klein, P. S. (2003). Toddlers' self-regulated compliance to mothers, caregivers, and fathers: Implications for theories of socialization. *Developmental Psychology, 39*(4), 680–692. doi:10.1037/0012-1649.39.4.680

Ferjan Ramirez, N., & Kuhl, P. (2017). Bilingual baby: Foreign language intervention in Madrid's infant education centers. *Mind, Brain, and Education, 11*(3), 133–143. doi:10.1111/mbe.12144

Flaugher, P. (2006). Two dimensions of parent participation in an inner school district. *Education and Urban Society, 38*(2), 248–261. doi:10.1177/0013124505284292

Foucault, M. (1980). *Power-knowledge: Selected Interviews and Other Writings 1972–1977.* New York, NY: Random House.

Fracasso, M. P., & Busch-Rossnagel, N. A. (1992). Parents and children of Hispanic origin. In M. E. Procidano & C. B. Fisher (Eds.), *Contemporary families: A handbook for school professionals* (pp. 83–98). New York, NY: Teachers College Press.

Garner, P. W., & Waajid, B. (2012). Emotion knowledge and self-regulation as predictors of preschoolers' cognitive ability, classroom behavior, and social competence. *Journal of Psychoeducational Assessment, 30*(4), 330–343. doi:10.1177/0734282912449441

Gruber, O., & Goschke, T. (2004). Executive control emerging from dynamic interactions between brain systems mediating language, working memory and attentional processes. *Acta Psychologica, 115,* 105–121. doi:10.1016/j.actpsy.2003.12.003

Halgunseth, L., Peterson, A., Stark, D. R., & Moodie, S. (2009). *Family engagement, diverse families, and early childhood education programs: An integrated review of the literature.* Washington, DC: NAEYC and Pre-K Now. https://nieer.org/wp-content/uploads/2011/09/EDF_Literature20Review.pdf

Hoover-Dempsey, K. V., Walker, J. M. T., Sandler, H. M., Whetsel, D., Green, C. L., Wilkins, A. S., & Closson, K. (2005). Why do parents become involved? Research findings and implications. *The Elementary School Journal, 106*(2), 105–130. doi:10.1086/499194

Ispa, J. M., Fine, M. A., Halgunseth, L. C., Harper, S., Robinson, J., Boyce, L., & Brady-Smith, C. (2004). Maternal intrusiveness, maternal warmth, and mother-toddler relationship outcomes: Variations across low-income ethnic and acculturation groups. *Child Development, 75,* 1613–1631. doi:10.1111/j.1467-8624.2004.00806.x

Keyser, J. (2006). *From parents to partners building a family-centered early childhood program.* St Paul, MN: Redleaf Press.

Kim, Y., Calzada, E. J., Barajas-Gonzalez, R. G., Huang, K.-Y., Brotman, L. M., Castro, A., & Pichardo, C. (2018). The role of authoritative and authoritarian parenting in the early academic achievement of Latino students. *Journal of Educational Psychology, 110*(1), 119–132. doi:10.1037/edu0000192

Kochanska, G. (2001). Emotional development in children with different attachment histories: The first three years. *Child Development, 72*(2), 474–490. doi:10.1111/1467-8624.00291

Kuczynski, L., & Kochanska, G. (1990). Development of children's noncompliance strategies from toddlerhood to age 5. *Developmental Psychology, 26*(3), 398–408. doi:10.1037/0012-1649.26.3.398

Ladson-Billings, G. (1995). Toward a theory of culturally relevant pedagogy. *American Educational Research Journal, 32*(3), 465–491. doi:10.1016/j.lindif.2009.07.002

Leung, C. B., & Brice, A. E. (2013). Ethical issues in conducting research with bilingual/dual language learners. In C. S. Rhodes & K. S. Weiss (Eds.), *Ethical issues in literacy research* (pp. 41–53). New York, NY: Routledge.

Liew, J. (2012). Effortful control, executive functions, and education: Bringing self-regulatory and social-emotional competencies to the table. *Child Development Perspectives, 6*(2), 105–111. doi:10.1111/j.1750-8606.2011.00196.x

Liew, J., McTigue, E. M., Barrois, L., & Hughes, J. N. (2008). Adaptive and effortful control and academic self-efficacy beliefs on achievement: A longitudinal study of 1st through 3rd graders. *Early Childhood Research Quarterly, 23*(4), 515–526. doi:10.1016/j.ecresq.2008.07.003

Lin, H., Lawrence, F. R., & Gorrell, J. (2003). Kindergarten teachers' views of children's readiness for school. *Early Childhood Research Quarterly, 18*(2), 225. doi:10.1016/S0885-2006(03)00028-0

Long Island Index. (2013). *2013 Long Island Index.* Garden City, NY: The Rauch Foundation.

Luchtel, M., Hughes, K., Luze, G., Richardson Bruna, K., & Peterson, C. (2010). A comparison of teacher-rated classroom conduct, social skills, and teacher-child relationship quality between preschool English learners and preschool English speakers. *NHSA Dialog, 13*(2), 92–111. doi:10.1080/15240751003737877

McClelland, M. M., Acock, A. C., & Morrison, F. J. (2006). The impact of kindergarten learning-related skills on academic trajectories at the end of elementary school. *Early Childhood Research Quarterly, 21*(4), 471–490. doi:10.1016/j.ecresq.2006.09.003

McClelland, M. M., Cameron, C. E., Connor, C., Farris, C. L., Jewkes, A. M., & Morrison, F. J. (2007). Links between behavioral regulation and preschoolers' literacy, vocabulary, and math skills. *Developmental Psychology, 43*(4), 947–959. doi:10.1037/0012-1649.43.4.947

McFadyen-Ketchum, L. S., Hurwich-Reiss, E., Stiles, A. A., Mendoza, M. M., Badanes, L. S., Dmitrieva, J., & Watamura, S. E. (2016). Self-regulation and economic stress in children of Hispanic immigrants and their peers: Better regulation at a cost? *Early Education and Development, 27*(7), 914–931. doi:10.1080/10409289.2015.1036345

McWayne, C. M., Melzi, G., Schick, A. R., Kennedy, J. L., & Mundt, K. (2013). Defining family engagement among Latino Head Start parents: A mixed-methods measurement development study. *Early Childhood Research Quarterly, 28*(3), 593–607. doi:10.1016/j.ecresq.2013.03.008

REFERENCES

Mendez Smith, J., & Vega, C. (2015). *Parent-teacher conferences for Hispanic children and families*. National Research Center on Hispanic Children and Families. Retrieved on December 27, 2015, from http://www.childtrends.org/?nrcblog-post=parent-teacher-conferencesfor-hispanic-children-and-families

Miller, E., & Almon, J. (2009). *Crisis in the kindergarten: Why children need to play in school*. College Park, MD: Alliance for Childhood.

Molfese, V. J., Modglin, A. A., Beswick, J. L., Neamon, J. D., Berg, S. A., Berg, J., & Molnar, A. (2006). Letter knowledge, phonological processing, and print knowledge: Skills development in nonreading preschool children. *Journal of Learning Disabilities, 39*(4), 296–305.

Muller, U., Jacques, S., Brocki, K., & Zelazo, D. (2009). The executive functions of language in preschool children. In A. Winsler, C. Fernyhough, & I. Montero (Eds.), *Private speech, executive functioning, and the development of verbal self-regulation* (pp. 53–68). New York, NY: Cambridge University Press.

Murray, K. T., & Kochanska, G. (2002). Effort control: Factor structure and relation to externalizing and internalizing behaviors. *Journal of Abnormal Child Psychology, 30*(5), 503–514.

Murray-Chandler, L. (2009). *Agent and subject of discipline: How novice teachers experience techniques of power* (Doctoral dissertation). ProQuest Dissertations and Theses. (UMI 3372135)

Nadeem, E., Maslak, K., Chacko, A., & Hoagwood, K. E. (2010). Aligning research and policy on social-emotional and academic competence for young children. *Early Education & Development, 21*(5), 765–779. doi:10.1080/10409289.2010.497452

New York State Prekindergarten Learning Standards. (2011). *New York State Prekindergarten Foundation for the Common Core*. Retrieved from http://www.p12.nysed.gov/ciai/common_core_standards/pdfdocs/nyslsprek.pdf

Perner, J., Lang, B., & Kloo, D. (2002). Theory of mind and self-control: More than a common problem of inhibition. *Child Development, 73*(3), 752–767.

Pettygrove, D., Hammond, S., Karahuta, E., Waugh, W., & Brownell, C. (2013). From cleaning up to helping out: Parental socialization and children's early prosocial behavior. *Infant Behavior & Development, 36*(4), 843–846. doi:10.1016/j.infbeh.2013.09.005

Raver, C. C., Jones, S. M., Li-Grining, C., Zhai, F., Bub, K., & Pressler, E. (2011). CSRP's impact on low-income preschoolers' preacademic skills: Self-regulation as a mediating mechanism. *Child Development, 82*(1), 362–378. doi:10.1111/j.467-8624.2010.01561.x

Rimm-Kaufman, S. E., Curby, T. W., Grimm, K. J., Nathanson, L., & Brock, L. L. (2009). The contribution of children's self-regulation and classroom quality to children's adaptive behaviors in the kindergarten classroom. *Developmental Psychology, 45*(4), 958–972. doi:10.1037/a0015861

Sibley, E., & Dearing, E. (2014). Family educational involvement and child achievement in early elementary school for American-born and immigrant families. *Psychology in the Schools, 51*(8). doi:10.1002/pits.21784

Smith, J., Stern, K., & Shatrova, Z. (2008). Factors inhibiting Hispanic parents' school involvement. *The Rural Educator, 29*(2), 8–13. doi:10.35608/ruraled.v29i2.468

Smith-Donald, R., Raver, C. C., Hayes, T., & Richardson, B. (2007). Preliminary construct and concurrent validity of the preschool self-regulation assessment (PSRA) for field-based research. *Early Childhood Research Quarterly, 22,* 173–187. doi:10.1016/j.ecresq.2007.01.002

Spinella, M., & Miley, W. (2004). Orbitofrontal function and educational attainment. *College Student Journal, 38*(3), 333–338.

Tabors, P. O., & López, L. M. (2005). How can teachers and parents help young children become and stay bilinguals? In J. David & M. Monsour (Eds.), *Head Start Bulletin: English language learners* (p. 14–17). Washington, DC: U.S. Department of Health and Human Services.

Tominey, S. L., & McClelland, M. M. (2011). Red light, purple light: Findings from a randomized trial using circle time games to improve behavioral self-regulation in preschool. *Early Education and Development, 22*(3), 489–519. doi:10.1080/10409289.2011.574258

Ursache, A., Blair, C., & Raver, C. (2012). The promotion of self-regulation as a means of enhancing school readiness and early achievement in children at risk for school failure. *Child Development Perspective, 6*(2). 122–128. doi:10.1111/j.1750-8606.2011.00209.x

Vitaro, F., Brendgen, M., Larose, S., & Tremblay, R. E. (2005). Kindergarten disruptive behaviors, protective factors, and educational achievement by early adulthood. *Journal of Educational Psychology, 97*(4), 617–629. doi:10.1037/0022-0663.97.4.617

Vygotsky, L. (1978). *Mind in society: The development of higher psychological processes.* Cambridge, MA: Harvard University Press Publications.

Wanless, S. B., McClelland, M. M., Tominey, S. L., & Acock, A.C. (2011). The influence of demographic risk factors on children's behavioral regulation in prekindergarten and kindergarten. *Early Education and Development, 22*(3), 461–488. doi:10.1080/10409289.2011.5361

Willoughby, M., Kupersmidt, J., Voegler-Lee, M., & Bryant, D. (2011). Contributions of hot and cool self-regulation to preschool disruptive behavior and academic achievement. *Developmental Neuropsychology, 36*(2), 162–180. doi:10.1080/87565641.2010.549980

Winsler, A., Fernyhough, C., & Montero, I. (2009). *Private speech, executive functioning, and the development of verbal self-regulation.* Cambridge, NY: Cambridge University Press.

Wood, L. E., & Grau, J. M. (2018). Associations between maternal control and child defiance among Puerto Rican-origin adolescent mothers and their toddlers: A person-centered examination. *Journal of Latina/o Psychology, 6*(4), 264–275. doi:10.1037/lat0000120

Yolanda Medina and Margarita Machado-Casas
Series EDITORS

Critical Studies of Latinxs in the Americas is a provocative interdisciplinary series that offers a critical space for reflection and questioning what it means to be Latinxs living in the Americas in twenty-first century social, cultural, economic, and political arenas. The series looks forward to extending the dialogue to include the North and South Western hemispheric relations that are prevalent in the field of global studies.

Topics that explore and advance research and scholarship on contemporary topics and issues related with processes of racialization, economic exploitation, health, education, transnationalism, immigration, gendered and sexual identities, and disabilities that are not commonly highlighted in the current Latinx Studies literature as well as the multitude of socio, cultural, economic, and political progress among the Latinxs in the Americas are welcome.

To receive more information about CSLA, please contact:

Yolanda Medina (ymedina@bmcc.cuny.edu) &
Margarita Machado-Casas (Margarita.MachadoCasas@utsa.edu)

To order other books in this series, please contact our Customer Service Department at:

peterlang@presswarehouse.com (within the U.S.)
order@peterlang.com (outside the U.S.)

Or browse online by series at:

WWW.PETERLANG.COM

www.ingramcontent.com/pod-product-compliance
Lightning Source LLC
Chambersburg PA
CBHW061720300426
44115CB00014B/2766